Sharon Tate Campaign Plan
MMXX

THE BOOK YOU ARE
ABOUT TO READ WILL
IMPART A RARE AND
UNIMAGINED SENSE
OF JOYFULNESS TO
YOU ABOUT SHARON
TATE AS A PERSON

Sharon Tate Campaign Plan MMXX

The Result of a Deliberative Process that Contemplates a New Dawn in Hollywood

First Edition

Michael A. Walker

A Magisterial Press Book

Sharon Tate Campaign Plan MMXX

The Result of a Deliberative Process that
Contemplates a New Dawn in Hollywood

Copyright © 2018 by Michael A. Walker
Magisterial Press

ISBN: 978-0-9996737-1-3 (Paperback)
ISBN: 978-0-9996737-2-0 (Hardcover)
ISBN: 978-0-9996737-3-7 (eBook)
ISBN: 978-0-9996737-4-4 (Audiobook)

Library of Congress Control Number: 2019900882

All Rights Reserved

Cover Photo:
Photographer Philippe Le Tellier/Paris
Match Archive/Getty Images

Magisterial Press is an Imprint
Alabaster, Alabama

First Magisterial Press Printing, January 1, 2019

Printed in the United States of America

Dedication

Doris Gwendolyn Tate
1924-1992

Doris fought with everything she had left to uphold justice for the murder of Sharon with the child she was expecting

Table of Contents

Acknowledgements xi
Foreword 1
Preamble 13
Preface 35
Introduction 57
Statement of the Purpose 69
Rationale 73
Assessment 87
The Plan 113
Timing 127
Conclusion 137
Annex A 141
Annex B 146
Annex C 148
Annex D 150
Appendix 1 to Annex D 152
Appendix 2 to Annex D 157
Index 161

"The Tate Family is on the way to Italy"
A Western Union Telegram from Doris Tate

© Michael A. Walker / All Rights Reserved

"I think something more powerful than we are decides our fates for us"

Sharon Tate

▶ **VISITS BANK** — With Dorothy Friday of Executive is her cousin, Sharon Tate, recently returned from Vicenza, Italy, to make her home in Houston. For the past two years, Sharon has made her home in Italy where her father is an officer with the U. S. Army.

Acknowledgements

I am thankful beyond measure for family and friends in life that permit me to research and write about topics of interest these days because they are being quite patient. Most of all I am indebted to my wife Ruth, and acknowledge the influence of the many professional acquaintances from various disciplines that are simply too numerous to mention in one place. Every last one of them unknowingly played a decisive role in showing me what right looks like by how they conducted their lives and work.

It is a privilege to have George Vreeland Hill writing the Foreword to this book. He really adds a colorful element needed to offset the necessary but grueling science of planning. I had never written to George before but one day decided to approach him as a public Sharon Tate advocate who had done some thinking about how to present her with dignity. We are but mere individuals who study Sharon Tate as a person, looking at the various issues encountered along the way. George thinks of one thing and I think of another, so there must be a way to collaborate with people on the Sharon Tate enigma. It is a fair guess that there are many more people out there that have something constructive to offer that actually advances Sharon Tate in the right direction.

After introducing myself, I described what I was working on to George, asked him if he would write something positive to go in the book's front matter and he agreed, so I wanted to acknowledge that to people here as an encouragement to further action. If you have not met George before he is a treasure-trove of interesting details and information about historical Hollywood as well as many of its greatest celebrities. It is purely speculative on my part but if Sharon were alive today, George Vreeland Hill would be her agent since after all he is Christina Aguilera's favorite person. George is also an excellent example of civics in action. He explores the people and places around Los Angeles many of which were also part of Sharon's life. I was struck by George's subject matter expertise concerning Sharon Tate, his love of country, as well as his public awareness efforts that continue to honor Sharon's memory. George relayed his excitement about the project when he heard about it and has been an encouragement ever since.

Acknowledgement also goes to the many writers and movie producers working on this topic which were more or less informative. These professionals had influences here and there leading to the development of this plan. Essential to everything this book addresses are the many ordinary individuals who may or may not know one another, and are seeking to find ways that will educate the public about Sharon Tate the right way. No matter how small you think your contribution might be, if it really is helpful to preserving Sharon's dignity, there are people that will appreciate you and it will have a net positive effect.

Acknowledgement is in order for the authorities that look out for our well-being and endure what can seem to be a thankless task. As I began to write, I quickly realized that if it were not for the authorities exercising the full extent of the various resources available to them, this entire episode could have turned out much worse. All citizens should acknowledge that the authorities are to be an agent for good in our world, and they exist to actively suppress evil. Despite confusion, debate, and hairsplitting at times, the system is considerably stable and works exceptionally well when you have the right people in power.

The original concept presented here began over twenty years ago as a flash of inspiration. However, unpacking, translating, and communicating that concept would turn out to be more like an accretion of bits and pieces over time. Obstacles encountered along the way were dismantled and eventually overcome. A workable, comprehensive solution began to gel only recently. Determination to finally sit down and compose this manuscript came after making personal contact with several careerist Hollywood actors who had nothing directly to do with this case other than hearing about it in a similar fashion to the average American. There is an undercurrent of some type among professional actors and workers in Hollywood who want to do something about the Sharon Tate situation. To me, it was exciting to communicate with the actors themselves because it suggests possibilities.

I also want to take a rare opportunity to publically acknowledge the work of Debra Ann Tate in her 2014 book *Sharon Tate: Recollection*[1] as a milestone achievement. Hers would be a closer approximation to what I try to describe in so many words here. *Sharon Tate: Recollection* is both informative and encouraging because its intent is to be a cheerful, positive account of Sharon's life apart from what has been an ocean of morbidity. This book is an outsider's presentation composed by a complete stranger to Debra, and I can only hope she considers authoring a subsequent and honed-in on Sharon encore performance for the general public in a volume that takes the best parts of that first effort of hers to a new level. I wish there were some other way than discussion of this ordeal to just say hello, but then again Sharon can act as a uniting force that brings people together in new ways. In the past, people befriended Debra for the wrong reasons so it takes time for her

---

1 Tate, D. (2014). *Sharon Tate: Recollection*. Running Press. Philadelphia, Pennsylvania, United States. ISBN: 9780762452354.

to figure folks out. I can still accept Debra from a distance, and recognize her right to criticize this work as it pertains to her. We are all grownups but have to remember that it is after all *her* family that God gave to her.

All fifty states now benefit from Doris Tate's work for Sharon, and it is on some profound level that Doris is made our gal from what she entrusted and unselfishly gave to all of us. I wish there were a way to thank Doris for her contribution and sheer resolve, but carrying on her work into the future is honors enough when done in her memory. Most of all, *Sharon Tate: Recollection* conveys an important aspect about Sharon's life that a lot of people may not yet be aware of: The literally millions of Sharon Tate images that exist. Needless to say, Debra exhibited some rather gifted insight into how to look at the problem. It is easy to forget that Debra is a unique person apart from her sister because of their resemblance, but I think of Debra often because she produced a loving book about one of her family members. It would be nice if we lived in a world where brothers and sisters loved one another as much.

Ultimately, I want to acknowledge my mother, Barbara. She was a character, and that is who God gave me in life, so she was perfect. Aside from the shocking news of these murders which caused a disturbance to our normal pattern of life all those years ago, it was my mom from whom I first ever learned of something unique about Sharon Tate as a person.

Dave Draper Catches Sharon Tate in the Movie *Don't Make Waves*

Photo / mptvimages.com

"Sexiness is all in the eye of the beholder"
Sharon Tate

Sharon Tate at the Microphone outside the Rivoli Theater in Myrtle Beach, South Carolina to Promote the Opening of *Don't Make Waves*

Courtesy of Jack Thompson / All Rights Reserved

Foreword

Sharon Tate – the mere mention of her name conjures up images of beauty, being free, Hollywood, and the 1960s. Her life was a short one; only 26 years, but she left her mark on us all. In the years since her passing, much has been said and written about the end of her life. Movies have portrayed her as a victim of a cult. However, Sharon was much more. She was an actress and model who started out in Hollywood with small parts in television shows such as *The Beverly Hillbillies* and *The Man from U.N.C.L.E.*, then graduated to the big screen.

She appeared in a number of films with her most notable role being as Jennifer North in Valley of the Dolls. Her best looking role was in Don't Make Waves as her eye-popping figure caught the eyes of many. Sharon was an up-and-comer who was being compared to the likes of Marilyn Monroe and Jayne Mansfield. Fame though, never really fazed her. She was a well-rounded girl who had a lot of different experiences growing up. Born in Dallas, Texas in 1943 to Colonel Paul Tate and his wife Doris, her parents saw the potential in Sharon that the world would eventually see. They entered their daughter in a beauty contest at the age of six months. Sharon won and became Miss Tiny Tot of Dallas.

Not a bad start for this new beauty. However, Paul, being in the Army, was transferred several times as Sharon would wind up living in the State of Washington, Italy, and other places. Despite all this moving, she kept her focus on life and wanted to go to college to study psychiatry. Sharon also kept her eye on modeling and even looked at the possibility of film work. That chance came in Italy when a Paul Newman film was being made nearby where she had a bit part. She even worked with Pat Boone in Venice. Returning to the United States to continue her studies, Sharon kept thinking about being an actress. Her father would soon be transferred again and this time, the Tate family would move to California.

Luck was always with Sharon. However, she never gloated about it. With two younger sisters, Sharon was a busy but loving family member. With her, family was always first. There was always time for the other things. This was the early 1960s. The Kennedy years – a new era of space travel was dawning and music was changing. The Beatles would soon conquer America. Culture was changing, and women were freer to do more things. Sharon, being a woman of the times, was in an age that was meant for her. She was a natural.

As those bit parts became bigger parts, her co-stars would often remark about how nice Sharon was or that she was a breath of fresh air. She was simply a joy to work with. As a result, her fan base grew and that included other Hollywood celebrities and directors. Her fan base kept on growing as well. Sharon was society and yet, she was a hippie. She had boyfriends and even lived with noted hairstylist, Jay Sebring. That relationship ended when Sharon met Roman Polanski, and would in time marry him. As more film work came her way, Sharon became pregnant.

Still the family oriented woman, she looked forward to the birth of her child. As we all know, that birth never came. The 1960s was also a time of experimenting and that meant drugs. A counterculture grew with defiant young people who no longer accepted the norm. It was an era of protests, and a very unpopular war. Cults grew, and out of nowhere came a man named Charles Manson. A slick con artist, he knew how to use people from his years in prison. Manson found San Francisco the epicenter of the hippie movement. He would gather followers of lost people who were searching for answers in an ever-changing environment. They drifted around, and settled in Los Angeles.

Manson wanted to be a famous musician. That never happened, so he took his frustrations out on those who accomplished what he could not. Murder was the result, and lives were snuffed out before their prime. One of those lives was Sharon Tate. She was a woman who should have seen many more tomorrows. However, she now gained fame in death that she wanted to achieve in life. A trial followed and so did a great deal of publicity, but who was the real Sharon? Should we care? Ask her fans who are countless around the world.

For example, George E. Smith is a Sharon Tate collector and historian who wrote four books about her, including *The House of Sharon Tate*[2] *and 10050 Cielo Drive*. He wrote the following for this introduction:

> "Many people have asked me over the years why I like Sharon Tate so much, what makes her so special to me. Well! My answer has always been she just makes me smile. Sharon Tate has been a part of my life since I was eleven years old, now I am sixty-two and she is still a very large part of my life.
>
> I first saw Sharon in a movie called *Don't Make Waves* and from that point on she has been my favorite movie star. Sharon was a person of the 'now' and also in my opinion, ahead of her time. Sharon was a kind person that loved her family and also loved animals. Sharon had a kindness and warmth few people in Hollywood have. Sharon Tate will always have a

---

[2] Smith, G. (2010). *The House of Sharon Tate*. Hardcover, 111 pages, signed by the author. Book size is 8"x11". **Note:** The book is unpublished and intended for collectors. For further information you can write Mr. Smith at the following address: Georges3@cox.net

very special place in my heart. My one wish is that I could have had the chance to meet her."

—George E. Smith

This book delves deep into Sharon's life and is for her fans who want to feel closer to her and also for those millions of fans yet to come who will discover this woman of the 1960s who is very much a part of the 2000s because of the Internet, and an ever growing interest as more and more books and films come out about her as well as the events surrounding her life. Yes, Sharon was always a girl of the times. I have been a fan of hers for decades. I remember my parents and grandmother going to see Valley of the Dolls. They left me and my brother and sister with our aunt because they felt we were too young to see a movie like that.

It would not be long before I fell in love with this actress who was a lot more than looks. Sharon was a giving person who always had time for her fans. There was nothing stuck-up about her. She loved animals and her home in Benedict Canyon was slowly turning into a zoo with cats, dogs and other furry things. There is that iconic photo of her feeding a goat. She loved doing those things. That was the real Sharon Tate. This book was written to show that. From humble beginnings to stardom, she never changed. It is sad that she has been portrayed in ways that are false. From rumors to lies, her life has sometimes been twisted in ways that has been bad for her image. Her fans know better.

Ernest Perrone of Central Valley, New York, a longtime friend and an even longer time fan of Sharon said:

> "Sharon gave a part of her soul to the movies, but she gave her whole heart to others. She was so loving and giving. That was the real Sharon Tate."
>
> *—Ernest Perrone*

Yes, this book captures what her fans have always known. She was beautiful both inside and out and she never hurt a soul or let anyone down. You can go anywhere online and see the loving tributes to her. From Facebook to YouTube to virtually every part of social media, you will see that fans will no longer tolerate the falseness and can see through it all. All truth comes out in time. As you read this book, you will be captivated from the start. As a fan, you will read it more than once.

My sister Diane Hill can't wait for this book. She said "I look forward to the book because I remember her and still enjoy the movies." Those movies are indeed still watched and enjoyed by people around the globe. Diane went on to write:

> "The 1960's saw the most rapid cultural changes than any other decade in post war America. It was a time like no other as we saw the best and the worst: Assassinations, riots coast to coast, Vietnam, and drug culture. The landscape of that era changed almost overnight after the summer of 1967. The 'Summer of Love' brought huge changes in pop culture via fashion, attitudes, music, hippies, 'Be-Ins', and 'Love- Ins'. It was incredible to live through that exceptional time. Through it all we witnessed mankind's greatest scientific achievement that would see American astronauts land on the Moon on that summer day in 1969. For one brief moment the world came together. Through that amazing time, no one could have predicted the horror that would take place on Cielo Drive in Los Angeles that August night in 1969 when Charles Manson ordered his followers to kill the residents there. Beautiful actress Sharon Tate, her unborn son, and her guests staying at the house were victims of the senseless murders. All had been robbed of their bright futures ahead. Two other victims of the "Manson Family" were brutally slain the following night. This terrifying crime spree spread a pallor of fear throughout Los Angeles that still exists. The freewheeling days of the late 60's

came to a tragic halt. The Age of Aquarius was over. As history puts it, Manson was the man who killed the 60's."

—Diane Hill

Here in Beverly Hills, they showed Valley of the Dolls in one of the theaters for the 50th anniversary of the film's release. The audience… packed. People want more. You are getting more as you read the pages to come. Sometimes you have to have to look at numbers and understand the motives of a machine like Hollywood in order to understand what the public sees in a celebrity. Often, the image is made up and our views are distorted, even though we may think otherwise. What was Sharon's real role in Hollywood? What did she want out of the whole picture? This book explains those questions and breaks it all down to a science.

Pay attention to the quotes. You are about to discover a lot more about the process of stardom and its effect on the future. You are about to read a book that uncovers more than you have ever read about before. A fan who wishes to be anonymous spoke of her own days in Hollywood trying to make it. She gave up her quest for stardom years ago, but spoke of how Hollywood can make or break someone with a dream. "Hollywood is hard. You can think you have something and then they spit you out. It can be rewarding, but so often it's heartbreaking. I don't know how Sharon Tate made it." This book will answer that. As I have already written … "It delves deep."

Several years after Sharon's murder, her mother, Doris Tate, would rise from the ashes of her mourning and start a victim's rights campaign that soon became a law. Doris wanted to change Sharon's unfair legacy from murder victim to symbol of victims' rights. To this day, it has made a difference and has given a voice to victims and their families. Hollywood today can look back at what people like Sharon Tate had to go through in order to get noticed, and progress as an actress. Hollywood is a dream for millions of people, but a reality for a few.

Sharon Groves, who was Sharon Tate's stunt double and friend in the movie *Don't Make Waves* had this to say:

> "I met Sharon Tate on the movie set of *Don't Make Waves*. Filming was taking place right on the beach in Malibu. I had been chosen by Tony Curtis to be her stunt double because we were both of the same stature.
>
> I remember the first order of business from the studio was for us to match perfectly in every way. We were given identical beige bikinis and make-up went to work on us head to toe. I was "too tan" and Sharon was "too light" so makeup was applied head to toe to balance out our skin tones. Sharon and I both found this amusing. I was given a very big blonde wig to hide my naturally dark hair. We were twins now. I climbed up onto the trampoline and began jumping warming up and doing flips.
>
> Sharon Tate showed up looking glamorous and wearing high heels and her bikini. She flipped those heels off and climbed up. I couldn't help but stare into her gorgeous, sunburst eyes. Tony Curtis was there on the sidelines to coach us. We weren't surprised because Tony often wanted to do his own stunts and the director appreciated this. Tony made us laugh so much with his jokes as we both showed Sharon how to jump for close-ups. Sharon and I agreed that Tony was the funniest actor on the set! He was truly funny.
>
> During the weeks ahead I showed Sharon how to jump off the trampoline into her movie boyfriend's arms. He was Dave Draper and he too was impressed with Sharon's coordination and gracefulness. The scene in the movie shows off Sharon's coordination perfectly. The following weeks we worked together in the surfing and beach scenes where Tony is run over with my surfboard and then he is dragged to the beach. Sharon was such a good sport during all this filming. During our lunch breaks the cast and I would enjoy dining on long tables of catered foods right on the beach. Sometimes

Sharon chose to invite her family to join her in her trailer for meals. Sharon missed Roman who was in Italy at the time and wanted her family's comfort.

 I was so lucky to work with Sharon Tate in *Don't Make Waves* and I will treasure this memory forever. I remember Sharon as stunningly beautiful, kind, soft spoken, with a sense of humor, graceful and talented. I hope she gets the Hollywood Star she deserves."

Sharon (Barker) Groves

From fans, celebrities and all those who knew Sharon, the tributes are endless. Well, why not? Sharon Tate is eternal. You will be fascinated by this book.

 I sure am.

George Vreeland Hill

© Lou Jacobs Jr. / mptvimages.com

"Politics is the womb
in which war develops"

Carl von Clausewitz

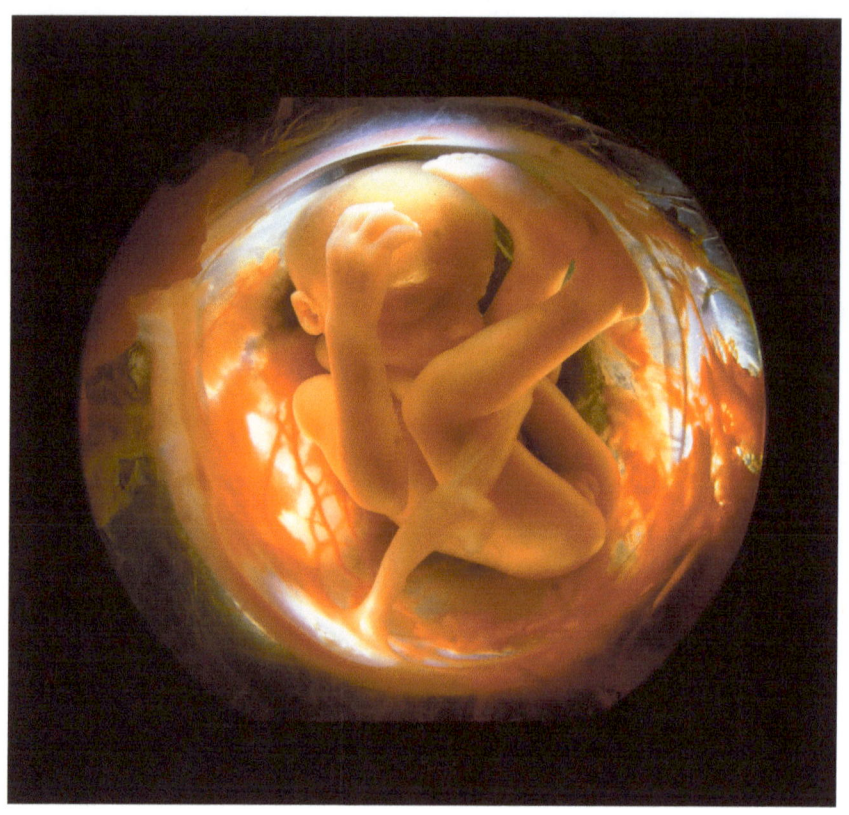

Lennart Nilsson / TT News agency

Preamble

Unless there is something factually new to report, the last thing anyone should want to do is put any more emphasis on a series of heinous acts carried out against our fellow citizens fifty years ago.[3] The way that the public came to learn what little they did of the people murdered in these crimes makes it a bit far-fetched at the moment to explore who they were in a normal manner. This campaign plan identifies the means of reintroducing Sharon Tate to the public.

The conviction of Charles Manson was a case application of the *vicarious liability rule of conspiracy* to commit murder and the penalty is exactly the same as it is for the ones physically carrying out the act.[4] That might sound technical, but the vicarious liability rule is akin to saying that whosoever hires or blackmails an assassin into acting will also be found guilty of murder as if he did it himself. Establishing motive is not essential for obtaining a vicarious liability rule of conspiracy to commit murder conviction.[5]

---

3 Torgerson, D. (August 10, 1969). Sharon Tate, Four Others Murdered. *Los Angeles Times*, pp. 1, 18.
4 Court of Appeals of California, Second Appellate District, Division One, August 13, 1976.
5 California Constitution, Article VI, § 13.

Given recent developments such as the death of Manson, accomplishing something balanced in portraying the lives of the innocent people he is guilty of murdering is now entirely within reach. Even full resolution is conceivable. This is done by simply reducing discussion of the crimes, the murderers, their accessories, attempted assassinations, and similar terrorist activities of the Manson Family or their advocates.

Exacting retribution remains a matter for the authorities to exercise on our behalf. A better way for the general public to dismantle Manson from American life is to first relegate him to the closet where he belongs. Final displacement of Manson is done through a public portrayal of someone worthy of admiration: Sharon Tate. Unless absolutely verified by more than one eyewitness or audio recordings as evidence, everything that was said or written since then attributed to Sharon or proves unhelpful to reclaiming her dignity is suspect. Any word ever uttered by the criminal fugitive Roman Polański since 1978 is inadmissible. We no longer link Manson with Sharon; we displace Manson with Sharon in the American psyche. If displacement were to occur, that moment in time would be a new dawn.

This book proposes a way forward to accomplish that end by promoting happy excerpts from the life of Sharon Tate and the elimination of clutter through an exclusionary lens. In support of this, nearly all cheerless discussion occurs early on in this book only as a means of touching on where we have been and how we got to where we are. Great lengths were taken in order for this presentation to narrow and genericize discussion of unhappy subjects, since they have been and will continue to be a potential pitfall in this case.

Nevertheless, seeing reality right-side up can understandably appear to be sanctimonious to persons who might be unaware of being stuck in a rut. This plan touches on explaining that condition or attitude, what causes it, why it persists, and yet despite all of this still show the pessimist a better way.

Unrelenting negativity without resolution in literature and movies is disfiguring to balanced narratives. Only where it becomes essential to make a point would any of the more leery issues from this case come up for discussion in the actual plan.

    This book also reports on the case with a detailed analysis in a completely different way than before. Accordingly, where references to unhappy topics do appear, it is with an eye to brevity and is intentionally infrequent. The emphasis is on characterizing a given problem related to Sharon Tate, and then presenting the problem's most potent solution. Sometimes reframing a complex problem occurs as a means to suggesting possibilities for further study. One purpose for touching on negativism at all in this book is to underscore the absurdity of maintaining the current trend. If it remains more popular than not to continually focus on ugliness, then that is a problem. We as a society need to go back and ask ourselves why that is.

    For many that were alive when Sharon Tate was still living, it is remarkable that our society pulled through that period. The country lost its sense of innocence. That sounds like an attempt at generalization since we tend to think more of an individual when it comes to innocence, but this plan takes the position that the actions of the individual will affect the community. This presentation dramatizes just how much that greater community suffered a catastrophic violation of innocence and continues to suffer from it to this day.

    The working thesis for the book is that our society is suffering from something akin to Stockholm syndrome when it comes to getting rid of the culture of death. Sharon Tate is at the epicenter of this loss of innocence and this book represents a proposal for extracting Sharon as someone surrounded and eventually attacked by evil from every side. The grip of evil on Sharon Tate continues to this day. Performing an extraction occurs through hindsight since Sharon is no longer alive, but it is still a valid means of rehearsing a rescue mission since evil persists in our world.

Such a social protection effort tailored for Sharon Tate must of necessity proceed from real charity, and the interested person has to know exactly what the word charity means. If this same cruelty happened to you, then you would expect charity to triumph when the time came for it even if it were done in your complete absence. For lack of descriptive adjectives, the violated people in our society are using the term "loss of innocence" to express a strong impression about the counterculture that exists within the greater American psyche.

The damage caused by the theft of innocence cannot be undone by those eventually found to be responsible. A murder cannot be undone by the criminal nor can the theft of innocence be undone by the criminal. The only recourse is a timely acknowledgement, yet patient retribution. Sometimes the sense of loss runs so deep that it can become a source of fighting strength or determination for a free and noble people. If you were not alive during the era Sharon lived, suffice it to say that it is one thing to read about that period of history, but it is quite another thing to actually live through it. The sense of loss was and is profound.

The idea in view is to at first relate where most Americans have been coming from regarding the subject of Sharon Tate. The better part of the American public's perception of Sharon today comes from the only readily available sources of information given to the public in the past. From there, the discussion leads the reader to more contemporary times in order to better understand the American psyche and examine pathways to resolution.

Part of that resolution is going to be learning from the counterculture delusion in all of its manifestations. First of all, at one point there was no counterculture and then quite suddenly, there it was. Its unchallenged propagation was about 36 months in duration. Somewhere within the turbulence of that timeframe, a culture of death emerged that was the counterculture's evil twin. It was a suspicious development, more seductive and subtle than anything but utterly exploitative in nature. Media was not particularly helpful when supporting or lending credibility to this evil twin's portrayal of itself as the more intelligent way of thinking. There was a great deal of conditioning to tolerate it going on. The conclusion from this survey is that the culture of death involves a seditious agenda to be ferreted out of our system no matter how irrational and complex it is found to be. No one in their right mind advocates a culture of death.

Sharon Tate paid for it with her life. Since then, all kinds of flimsy and unsubstantiated connections with the underworld were made about Sharon Tate. Some of the people around her only added to an increasingly negative impression, but Sharon Tate as a person was different. That concept may appear to be new to people who have already made up their minds about Sharon being hopelessly decadent like her murderers did. This campaign plan demonstrates beyond a shadow of a doubt the joyful place that the real Sharon Tate occupies and is still teaching us to this day about selfless commitment. It was always there, but she only rediscovered it in the last year of her life. Sharon's life blossomed into a genuine expression of class that contributes in a positive way to a culture of life. Sharon did this despite attempts at the personal level to manipulate her otherwise. That is her real story, and it always was triumphant whether or not anyone realizes it.

Since Sharon's death, the country often entertained and at times took the wrong path, allured by the culture of death's facile yet seductive enticements. In a culture of death, a few illegal drug overdose deaths mean nothing. Any responsible parties will probably not get caught, and the drug user probably never felt much pain going into cardiac arrest. After a while, legalization makes sense if you can be seduced enough to ignore the body count.

Another example of taking the wrong path is degradation as a public form of entertainment. That characterization is intentionally broad but people should consider the hard facts: Books and movies dwelled incessantly on Sharon's death, mesmerizing audiences with horrific acts of assault committed against her by a group of hippie-styled mass murderers. In turn, these negative portrayals of Sharon made a great deal of money for producers. Productions took those types of risks because the system allowed it and the producers attained their reward. In fact, more and more people were already inclined in that direction for their own entertainment. Apparently, Sharon looked tempting in other ways.

Audiences reliving Sharon's murder in ever more vivid detail highlight one symptom of an out of control show business syndicate. Her lopsided portrayal represents a helpless giant of an industry without adequate preventative measures. The present situation offers some clues about just how this conundrum of morbid death became a form of entertainment carrying on as it does. Situation ethics became the enabler because consumers of entertainment were voting for more gruesome accounts in motion pictures, theater, and literature with their dollars. Something happened to our culture, because the general public had never acted that way before. The counterculture arrived, and along with it a camouflaged culture of death, which is the enemy of free men and women everywhere.

The culture of death is an identifiable phenomenon allowed to propagate in our society with little constraint. In its earliest appearances, the hippies, yippies, and similarly disposed gangs claimed to be the know-it-alls of the counterculture world. Not all hippies were criminal. There were a lot of good people mixed up with these gangs. Socially, there was peer pressure to be either conformist or embrace a counterculture philosophical outlook. Social pressures in both directions were entrenched and perpetuated serious social division. Diffusion of that division would interfere with society going forward at a healthy pace, and divert significant public resources to combat its growing menace. The cost of policing the wasteful counterculture could have gone to the poor.

Metaphorically speaking, the culture of death's tentacles managed to grow enough to strike at society's vitals. This nuisance slithered back into hiding and began feeding in earnest off its host. Eventually the culture of death would corrupt society's institutions over a long period of time. There was a frequent demand for unquestioned and open tolerance of the culture of death. In major media, money could now be made from the real exploitation and degradation of our fellow citizens. There was an articulate ideology and corresponding agenda actively promoting a culture of death, and it is traceable. A lot of people suffered deception in thinking they were doing a good thing in going along with what is the defacement of genuine liberty in the name of freedom.

All sorts of ideologies wanted a stab at our society as well. Some ideologies were more digestible than others. A good example is humanism as the "new" social construct. On the one hand, humanitarian efforts such as life support and disaster relief are honorable. Charity is still of the highest social order. However, humanism is a sterile philosophical system that oftentimes weaponizes private forms of philanthropy because it is more frequently absent charity. Philanthropy can be inefficient because it often treats symptoms rather than problems. The problem is a lack of charity, not a lack of tolerance. For instance, healthy people do not need drugs. It may be philanthropic to provide subsidy to the drug culture out of a concern for giving drug users what they truly need, but subsidizing everything has nothing to do with charity. Equivocation of philanthropy and charity is rife among citizens.

Often masquerading as humanitarian, the system of humanism is an internally conflicted philosophy because humans are conflicted. It may sound obtuse to say that at first glance, but it directly applies to the case at hand. For someone like Manson to say he is both God and Satan at the same time is not only mistaken, it is the ultimate place that religious humanism leads. Manson fooled a lot of people with humanism. The man-centered philosophical system of humanism oftentimes facilitates the culture of death's agenda because everyone does what is right in their own eyes. An example of this is attempting to craft laws that legalize drugs on demand.

It is in a legal free-for-all that we now live whether we like it or not. As an established, separate system, humanism also carries with it an ability to propagate a concordant narrative. An example of this is people promoting in public the deliberate taking of innocent human life without negative consequence. In some examples, inferior laws allow this ugly behavior to go unchecked. It is genuinely humanitarian to restrict humanists or any other philosophical system from the ability to propagate a culture of death narrative in our society. There is a better way.

One might still wonder what all this has to do with a bunch of folks that one day saw nothing wrong with choosing death for innocent people. Another question to ask is what intensified conditions in our society that led to these murderers of Sharon Tate choosing death. That question will lead to exploring any connection between choosing and then acting upon that choice, as well as how that connection fits into the culture of death seduction. It does not matter who desires the homicidal choice because the outcome is the same. Sharon was different. All Sharon wanted was for her child to live, even at the expense of her own life. Ladies and gentlemen, that kind of statement does not come from the world.

In the bigger picture, the culture of death necessarily harbors hostile intent toward the story of someone like Sharon because she is a person who teaches us the sanctity of life. To some, smothering Sharon's story of life or outright maligning her in the aftermath of the crimes occurs because she poses a threat to the Mephistophelian culture of death's counter narrative. The reward for maligning Sharon's real life story is either monetary or from a mischievous exploitation of her stardom for impure purposes. Sharon was socially vulnerable, and practically made defenseless in the ensuing narrative. These social problems became entrenched in many institutions but are worth mentioning here only as a way of furthering public awareness and understanding. We can take a hard look at the symptoms of decadence to get past it, and seek what is good.

There are several new things to report about this crime in addition to outlining the culture of death's contours with a higher resolution. The culture of death as an outlook relies to a great extent upon seduction as the means, and the theft of innocence as its way. Seduction appears to be a frequent method of choice when devouring innocence, much like the many cases of murder where a child is enticed with candy or someone pretending to be friends lures the innocent away with a verbal enticement of some type to then violate their person. In both examples, the murderer is at first using philanthropic methods proceeding from a masked motive. In her own way, Sharon was vulnerable and it is necessary more than ever to address who the object of her affections really was in this case. The exploitation of vulnerability as a modus operandi is itself not new. However, reporting on this crime can explore the depths of Sharon's vulnerability as it relates to the intrusion of risk-laden seductive cultural influences of the time. Sharon and her child were that much more vulnerable to an assault, given the kind of change that was coming about.

Accusation first points toward the criminals and rightly so but the theft of innocence is also a significant evil and never explored in detail within a book about Sharon Tate. The allure of a beautiful woman being tied up and stabbed to death by a barbarian seems to spellbind people, and the system allows that to then be made into a movie. We also have the problem of misleading her and the corruption of Sharon as a person at various times, but homicidal choice is the ultimate violation of innocence. The deeper issue at hand is that something caused these crimes to even be entertained in the first place. Experts began studying the different ways that murderers experienced physiological pleasure during the commission of their crimes which was signaling reward to them for continuation of the behavior in the future. We do not need a movie to help them out. In Sharon's case, there is an illicit exercise of power over others involved, facilitated by the perpetrator's use of illegal drugs. We can consider connections to the *substantia nigra* part of the brain as an effect, but it will not establish the primary cause.

Looking at the offense from the inside out, Sharon's child was the most innocent and vulnerable person present at the scene of the crime. This is someone who would be aware of a loud crack of gunfire. There would be a dramatic increase in heartrate and breathing sensed in the darkness, distress might be sensed, but the curdling scream of the mother's voice with the sound of what was a knife being plunged repeatedly into her body would definitely be noticeable. Convulsions from each stab would no doubt lurch her baby around in the darkness. A sudden feeling of being horribly squashed would happen as Sharon's mortally wounded body then fell to the floor. The violation of Sharon Tate was now almost complete. Sharon's child would be the last to die at the scene of the crime.

Once the sensation of all the unusual commotion finally ceased, her baby would surely notice that the once constant and loud beating heart of Sharon was becoming erratic if not extremely faint. Sharon's heartrate would quickly slow from blood loss and come to a complete stop. The temperature would start to drop as the rate of circulation ebbed. A growing sense of suffocation caused by the oxygen supply being cut off would happen. A gurgling sound would start to come from Sharon's motionless torso.

Murder is the devil's business, and that night's macabre business would not be complete unless the death of Sharon's tiny, helpless baby occurred. The murderers apparently contemplated[6] how they might extract and further mutilate

---

6   Schiller, L. (1970). *The Killing of Sharon Tate*. Signet Books, New York, New York, United States. ISBN: 978-0451042583.

the still living body. If that does not make you angry then something is wrong. These murderers opted for a slow and agonizing death by simply walking away knowing what would happen to the only living human being left in the house. In the final moments, Sharon's child would go through a series of involuntary convulsions occurring from a last ditch attempt to find air, but finally the end would come. Six human beings died in the course of the mass murders that night. Sharon's child was at the forefront of her concerns but would also succumb to a morbid end, becoming a part of what millions of Americans still consider to be the most horrifying crime scene of the twentieth century. Once everyone was dead, there was silence. Welcome to the human race, Sharon Tate. Born in Dallas, Texas on January 24, 1943 at 5:47PM, Sharon Tate along with the child she was carrying suffered from a monstrous evildoing somewhere after midnight and 1:00AM on August 9, 1969.

Aside from the death penalty being struck down, one of the greatest injustices arising out of Sharon's case is that no charges of any type would be filed for prosecution of this particular offense against her child. That is a significant problem worth further detailed examination by the finest legal experts available. Finding a potential solution could result in a formal criminal complaint that would have the effect of suspending further parole applications until a decision authority issues its findings. Let us consider for a moment in the following paragraphs how a potential solution might actually play out.

The Los Angeles District Attorney's office initially looked into the question of the intentional homicide of Sharon's child in 1969. The prosecution needed the authority to act and began looking at laws on the books at that point in time. The result of the preliminary study found increasing complexity and ambiguity regarding what legal protection Sharon's child had under the constitution of the State of California. Prior to 1973 under the Constitution of the United States of America, Sharon's child has the right to life, liberty, and the pursuit of happiness like the rest of us. However, frustration with ambiguities encountered in the State of California's tangled labyrinth of legal precedents in 1969 would complicate and jeopardize the prosecution's swift and certain prosecution for the other murders committed that night. Given the situation of a mass murder, there appears to be a superficially acceptable degree of pragmatism by the prosecution for building its case without having a sixth murder charge available to enter for the entire set of August 9, 1969 murders. In Bugliosi's final summation to the jury he argued that, "in a very real sense, six murders occurred that night."[7] At that time, a conviction for any of the murders committed would have the same terminal effect when asking for the death penalty. The prosecution would go on to effect a spectacular application of the law for conspiracy to commit murder in one of the most legendary criminal cases in history.

There is no way that the prosecution could have known beforehand that in 1972 the death penalty would be struck down in California,[8] and that these criminals would start applying for parole shortly thereafter *based on the murders prosecuted*. Since then, the law strengthened so that prosecutors can file charges for intentional homicide in cases like the murder of Sharon's child. Even though the State of California later reenacted the death penalty, there was no retroactive aspect attached to the reinstatement referendum even though it took the form of a state constitutional amendment. Astonishingly, all previous murder convictions in California prior to 1972 received an immediate retroactive annulment of the death penalty without question. The persistent disarray caused by that retroactive annulment represents a significant issue that the average citizen honestly questions.

Let us look at the result of that 1972 decision striking down the death penalty for a moment. The authorities close down death

---

7   Bugliosi, V. & Gentry, C. (1974), *Helter Skelter: The True Story of the Manson Murders*. W. W. Norton & Company, New York, New York, United States. ISBN: 978-0393322231.

8   Supreme Court of California, *People versus Anderson*, February 12, 1972.

row and put the Manson murderers into regular jail cells, and Charles Manson goes on to become the prisoner with the most fan mail in the history of the United States, inspiring followers to commit further atrocities to include an assassination attempt on the President. Death penalty opponents do nothing about any of this because they are having things their way. There is something substantive to the public's dissatisfaction with the result, and there is a way to effectively confront the problem for which we will now explore. To begin the process, let us locate the offense and reframe the problem in terms that the public can understand.

Looking at this entire crime from the perspective of Sharon's child – as Sharon Tate did – there was not, nor will there be a homicide prosecution any time soon. The culture of death philosophy already succeeded in corrupting an institution to the point that it inflicted a mortal fifty year wound in a reign of terror against Sharon's child. The situation remains an insult to the sensibilities of the State of California's citizens to this day. In a very real sense, the proponents of judicial activism in 1972 likewise just walked away from Sharon's child letting any hope of a future prosecution for this particular murder hang in nothingness. The unintentional cruelty of death penalty opponents in this instance reached intolerable heights, and the people of California fought back with a referendum enacted in November, 1972. Something about the reimplementation of the death penalty in California later that year was insufficient.

What makes little sense is how striking down the death penalty in 1972 is to also be immediately retroactive. That in itself is an *outrage*. To be clear, there was zero retroactive application of the law made subsequent to the murder of Sharon's child even though there was already a reinstatement of the death penalty in California by that time. There is something hideously wrong with the entire situation. This plan envisions a simultaneous legal initiative to reverse this glaring injustice. Success with the proposed solution that follows depends on how deeply ingrained the Manson murders remain in the American public's consciousness. The first initiative would be a taskforce out of the California Attorney General's office with the potential of it becoming a joint taskforce under counterterrorism authorities. The second initiative would be a unified social and political pressure network to motion for a human life amendment to the Constitution of the United States. This is made possible by California's representatives in Washington, DC working in concert with the California Attorney General. The State of California does not have the power to introduce its own human life amendment.

At present, the counterargument is going to be the ill-defined State of California law in existence *at the time of the murder*. What that kind of vagueness in the law did was allow someone to deprive another human being of life without due process in clear violation of the US Constitution. In order to prevent this disarray from ever happening again, the only preventive measure available to citizens is a human life amendment to the US Constitution. The human life amendment would facilitate filing murder charges for Sharon's child in the State of California, and also protect expecting women from this hideous crime against their children in all fifty states. Furthermore, having a death penalty on the books in all fifty states for the act of first degree murder has favorable healthcare implications. Enough states support a human life amendment to the US Constitution to enact it, and lawmakers could introduce the motion in the next session of Congress. The facts are the facts: The taking of human life without due process occurs whenever there is intentional or unintentional ambiguity introduced into laws by reckless culture of death proponents.

Ratification of the human life amendment by individual state legislatures would still allow the death penalty to remain on the books for the crime of first degree murder in those states. A stipulation clause to the amendment would be that in the future, should any remaining state in the union pass into law a death penalty for acts of first degree murder committed within its jurisdiction, it would immediately become permanent *and retroactive* for any previous first degree murder convictions. This would result in the addition of a penalty phase hearing to previous first degree murder convictions by a jury of peers, requiring additional criminal justice system funding authorities to clear the docket. At this point, the 1972 death penalty annulment becomes effectively struck down by a human life amendment to the US Constitution. Until that happens, a special legal taskforce out of the California Attorney General's office is going to become a necessity in order to find the interim remedy for the murder of Sharon Tate's child.

Legal experts can explore these complexities in exhaustive detail, and publish a final determination for what the charges would consist of for murdering Sharon's child. This would occur before going through the motions of an additional criminal prosecution in the absence of a supporting US Constitutional Amendment. Citizens can briefly and respectfully request that the authorities find something that will stick on those responsible for murdering Sharon's child, and move on it. California citizens can ask their state representatives for help by writing to them with brevity, clarity, and in the most respectful tone of voice. State legislature staffers can cite counterterrorism funding authorities for markup, and have representatives introduce the measure at the next session in Sacramento.

For the legal taskforce interim solution, a series of persuasive articles written to the local newspaper editorial column would increase public awareness. Any public statement in support of this would bring additional pressure on state representatives to allocate the necessary funding in the next budget round to conduct a special inquiry of great public interest. The mission of the taskforce would be to identify with clarity that Sharon Tate's child was a constituent and is by definition found to be of a compelling interest to the State of California. The taskforce would also prescribe what legal authorities allow entering an intentional homicide charge of any type for this murder. As results emerge from the study such as the murderer's previously stated confession to this particular offense, momentum would build and serve as a prelude to approaching the Los Angeles District Attorney's office with a new homicide charge in the already famous case.

People that were once at philosophical odds with each other would out of mutual concern for justice in Sharon's case be able to join hands on a united front. The California legislature can earmark increased funding authorities for the purpose of setting up a taskforce headed by a high-profile and distinguished legal team. The Attorney General would handpick the members for appointment. If continued murder advocacy is deemed an act of terrorism intended to overthrow the government such as that continually perpetuated by many Manson Family murder advocates or groups such as the Weather Underground,[9] the Attorney General's office can directly request additional federal funding to pursue the discovery of charges for all involved under existing laws. This would make it a joint taskforce with the Los Angeles County District Attorney's office as lead agency. If this proposed solution was to play out as described, or some very similar scenario like it, the Tate family will finally attain some measure of justice for the murder of Sharon Tate's child.

Prestige would increase dramatically for the authorities looking further into this question regardless of the outcome, with the entire country taking interest and rallying in support. It would definitely be an avenue for the media's old glory days to go all out on another Manson Family related murder prosecution. The message would be quite clear: If you commit murder, the authorities will relentlessly pursue you with every instrument of power entrusted to them by the people. This issue was ever so near to Sharon's heart, but since she died Sharon

---

9   The American Spectator (November 21, 2017). *Let's not forget Bernardine Dohrn, Bill Ayers, and the Four-Finger Salute.* Alexandria, Virginia, United States.

needs someone to be that voice in her place. Why is it that some people cannot really see she was pregnant?

The answer to that question is at least in part due to the unrestrained propagation of a culture of death philosophy throughout society by anachronistic persons who may, or may not realize what they are doing. The filing of a new charge is worth exploring based on the physical evidence attained from the scene of the crime, as well as the recorded confessions of the murderers. It is a complete violation of life, a rejection of all the scientific facts, an obstinate denial of reality by some people, a willful blindness to the overwhelming physical evidence, *and all that is good* to avoid this clear offense against Sharon's child.

The law at that point in time seemed vague enough to act as if the murder of Sharon's child was not a homicide, so seeking provisions in the penumbra of the law that effectively treats these idiosyncrasies is foreseeable. An antisocial and unscientific view of the unborn child was a relatively recent phenomenon in the history of our society which has run its course. The disarray of the times allowed advocates of the culture of death to run amok and have no mercy in bludgeoning or degrading the dignity of someone like Sharon Tate or her child.

Ambiguity in the law also allows degradation as entertainment to exist in many forms as well as giving encouragement for murder advocates to publically offend the sensibilities, with an air of impunity. That too is going to end. Sharon, if she were alive today, would certainly demand retribution by the authorities as well as authorization for a full-scale official inquiry into the culture of death's obfuscation, defective philosophy, modus operandi, and ultimate obstruction of justice. This is how due process and remedy for the murder of Sharon Tate's child could play out, and it is a win-win situation. There is strong public support backing reassertion of a culture of life given the scientific facts and the many corroborating technological improvements permitting the public to see what is going on. This outline and description of a potent and efficacious solution is what it would take to exact justice for Sharon's murdered child. The future indeed looks bright, thanks to the work of Doris Tate.

Today, society is becoming more cognizant of what exactly happened to cause this sense of a loss of innocence in the American psyche. However, we are in a far better position to combat and reverse it than before because of what Doris Tate did. We also now know what to look for in the future. There is today a greater understanding of what gives the more profane forms of seduction their allure, and why some people are more susceptible to it than others. Bad things happen on purpose or by mistake, and in the more healthy societies a pattern of learning usually takes place as a result. Sharon Tate offers something worthwhile for the public to learn from by studying what is good about her life in those places where it really counts. We will have grown as a society when we acquire wisdom about this case as it relates to the entire American experience.

This presentation is an optimistic campaign plan with a defined end state that studies a better way of ending one chapter in American history and starting the next on a stable footing. Out of over 37,000 words in an early draft of this manuscript, the name Manson appeared in only 59 places, 22 of which are only in reference to the Manson *Family*. However, Sharon had 669 direct references or 94 percent by comparison. Every instance of a Manson mention in this book is for the purpose of identifying and increasing public situational awareness of Manson's inferior philosophy. There are also situations that describe this plan's "steady state" that involves a study of Manson's diminishing ratios in proportion to Sharon Tate. One other place to seek elimination of Manson is to describe the end state, but it necessitates briefly mentioning Manson and his demise.

Maybe in the not too distant future, all books and movies about Sharon Tate will have zero Manson references. There are already examples of websites and books focused solely on positive and uplifting accounts of Sharon Tate's life appearing in print, as well as a new set of movies describing only her life that are in a production phase. To have a definable moment, Sharon Tate may well play her greatest role yet despite the theft of her life, innocence, and dignity. In the broader context there is a culture of death to deal with that our system is sluggish to recognize and suppress. Hopefully, a new dawn will emerge where Sharon Tate is known and appreciated more for who she is and not what was done to her.

"Pursue one great decisive aim with force and determination"

Carl von Clausewitz

First Man on the Moon July 21, 1969

Source: NASA

Preface

It was a day that I remember well. In disgust and totally out of the blue my mom suddenly threw a book she was reading down to the floor and everyone that was present immediately froze in their tracks. She then proceeded to strictly forbid anyone to read what would turn out to be a Vincent Bugliosi[10, 11] book about the Sharon Tate murders. My mom had never done something like that before, or since.

However, a movie[12] based on Bugliosi's book appeared on television only a year or two later. Curious as to whether or not the movie was a factual representation or overdramatized, I asked and eventually received conditional permission to read Bugliosi's book for the purpose of comparing it to the television movie. It took some convincing. Bugliosi's book was more real and therefore more horrible because to read it caused a creeping paranoia to develop about the people we live with in the world. Yet that was all anyone really had to go by at that point in time.

---

10 Vincent Bugliosi died June 6, 2015 in Los Angeles, California.
11 Bugliosi, V. & Gentry, C. (1974), *Helter Skelter: The True Story of the Manson Murders*. W. W. Norton & Company, New York, New York, United States. ISBN: 978-0393322231.
12 Lorimar Productions (1976). *Helter Skelter*. IMDb title tt0074621.

We tend to think that people are of themselves good within their core essence of being. This is not the case, and if it were so, there would be little need for laws. The only good thing gained from reading Bugliosi's book was to give more thought to the concept of discernment. I came to the conclusion that discernment is a necessary aspect of life that comes easily to some, but not at all to others. Discernment takes practice; much like playing a musical instrument takes practice.

For me, hippies were capable but irresponsible people who conspired to break the law out of cleverly disguised but selfish motives such as draft dodging. Hippies cheaply threw around high-sounding words but then became somewhat incoherent with their esoteric slang as if they were somehow more enlightened than anyone else could be. This came across as a non-threatening superiority complex in the more pronounced cases. I remember hippies as being easily led by a philosophy that came from the outside, whatever that outside was.

At first, I remained somewhat indifferent because I sensed that sooner or later hippies would find out what totalitarianism was like if they were just left to their own devices. Illegal drugs enslaved people, for starters. Hippies could seem gang-like to people who exercised caution in their associations. Most of the time you would see the police busting hippies, and that only spelled trouble to people that were at first accepting but not convinced enough of the hippie worldview to adopt it. Socially, hippies were frequently sneered at as undesirable types, and this was mostly because of their rampant drug abuse. Drugs were and are for remedying the sick, so the general public's impression of hippies at the time was not good. Drug abuse was understood to be an early indication of decadence setting in on a society.

Hippies considered persons who did not wish to go along with hippie counterculture to be judgmental or lacking understanding, but this was considerably off base. The invectives hurled by hippies were so loud and frequent that they became cliché after a while. These types of accusations became a strange sounding form of hippie judgmentalism arising out of its own. For a considerable period of time hippies were the most entrenched ideologues, driven mostly by a vision of some nondescript utopia. The thought of utopia seemed to touch hippie amygdalae in such a way that they simply could not bear to give in to realism. The beginnings of serious division within society occurred. Repeated failure to attain the envisioned utopia wound up being only more repeated failures for which society itself was to blame.

There were indeed problems with the world but not in the way that hippies condemned everyday society as dystopian. If anything, hippies that were relying on altered states of consciousness as the basis of reality were on the fast track to creating a real dystopia of their own. Hippie-style indiscretions and a totalitarian survival of the fittest outlook on life were one of the things wrong with the world. A more sobering form of intervention would be a good starting place to get hippies to face reality.

There was brashness. Hippies exaggerated the significance of their incantations, symbols, and hand gestures as if performing these identifying rites possessed attention-grabbing, internally therapeutic benefits. The hippie experience was great fodder for aspiring sociologists to write about. However, for political socialists without scruples, there was a zealous if not outright eager exploitation of hippie counterculture. Socialists tended to envision hippie counterculture as a beguiling, if not outright tantalizing platform from which the introduction of socialism into mainstream American society could occur.

For me, hippie rites were pretty much group-think and a contrivance lacking substance that sought to accomplish more than what it actually represented. It all seemed like "We the hippies are here so deal with it, and oh by the way, this stuff we are doing is a breakthrough that is totally new to human history and must be memorialized – just look at our works of art." In one respect, hippie mysticism, symbology and hand gestures were superficialities no different than Swastikas or Hitler salutes. Identifying the root cause was somewhat challenging, but one could reduce hippie counterculture to a handful of explanations.

Hippies were definitely trying to satisfy some kind of emptiness inside and a great many of the youth found intoxication in the very thought of striking out on their own earlier than normal. Hippies were numerous, and were experiencing a stronger sense of belonging from participation in hippie counterculture than they were getting from everyday society. Some hippies were suffering from simple attention deficit disorder and took the hippie way out as an available means of addressing the affliction.

In cases of utter despair or confusion, some hippies sensed something was wrong and turned to the church. There were a lot more hippies doing this than people realize. Hippie philosophy has an allure to it but does not satisfy the soul because at its very basis is a simple humanism where imperfect man is made the beginning and measure of all things. Since all people eventually die, there is something to be said about humanism's correlation with the culture of death. Redefinition of the word "peace" was underway to make it speak more intensely at the social and political levels of society. The church received hippies being drawn and communicated to them an altogether different peace – a peace that passes all human understanding.

There was a cost. Calculating the human cost of the counterculture would be difficult to pin down, but it was enormous. Additionally, an alarming trend was hippie philosophy that served as an entire replacement framework for real families. I could see where hippies were going with it though: If real families were unfulfilling to hippies, then a philosophical replacement framework provided them a substitute. Gangsterism satisfies the absence of real family and it gives gangs a kind of power from a sense of belonging.

Hippies dealt with disapproval in pretty much the same manner. A hippie receiving negative attention is perhaps better than no attention, as it were. Some developments were indications of a deeper exploitation of the counterculture by nefarious persons with an agenda. There were already some superficial indications of hippie replacement philosophy taking place. Cheap spray paint graffiti on already painted bridges and road signs seemed more to cover up something than to make a statement. To me, it had the veneer of vandalism. It seemed like a way to mask over what was from all appearances a form of barbarianism enabled by twentieth century technological achievement.

The hunch was not unfounded. Few hippies worked for a living. Parents had difficulty maintaining the slightest degree of rightful oversight. An aggravating factor was that the hippie philosophy and subculture aimed itself squarely at the youthful. Illegal drugs not only made hippies derelict, it made them addicts that posed a criminal threat to everyone – including their own families – in order to sustain a wretched stew of expensive and illegal chemical dependencies.

After reading Bugliosi's book, hippies were now murderers of innocent people. If that was not an accurate characterization, hippies were at least to blame for precipitating conditions that would lead to a devaluation of human life. Beyond the philosophical oddities, hippies had embarrassing misconceptions in the area of the political sciences. If hippies were so dead set against fascism, they certainly were cozy with its cousin, communism. Communism suited hippies better perhaps because the state owns you in that system and not the family.

Whether or not Sharon's murderers met the definition of hippies is a technicality, but they sure looked the part. This remains debatable because it is inexact as to whether hippie philosophy was coming from the generational divide or some other thing. Hippies certainly were part of the counterculture that did not want to participate or contribute from within the existing system. Accordingly, hippies could never shake off the perception of having a partial disconnect from reality because they were always trying to escape it. The philosophical outlook between the hippies and the broader counterculture movement was nearly identical. There was something ironic about it all.

Each page of Bugliosi's book[13] was worse than the page before. I was able to fill in some blanks to the whole story depicted in the television movie, and was at least getting a view of the bigger picture. Along with these impressions, I noticed after completing my comparative analysis that there was still scant information about Sharon Tate as a person. Sure, there was some basic data presented such as retracing some of Sharon's steps prior to the murder and some rather vague, overgeneralized information as to her personality.

As time went by there was news about releasing Sharon's murderers from prison, which was not an entirely unexpected development. However, it caused alarm about the rate of decline going on within our justice system. I sensed that something had to be done about it by the old guard who would come out of retirement, step in, crack some knuckles, and restore public confidence in the institution. For convicts, there were only four possibilities: 1) wrongly convicted, 2) activists making conscientious sacrifices, 3) mental cases, or 4) just plain evil persons.

It was later in life that I ran across a paperback at a garage sale that was written by one of Sharon's murderers and I immediately thought back to those days of yesteryear. I did not know what to make of this book after reading it, so instead I decided to play detective. I went back and re-read Bugliosi's book to compare it to this account, as well as to the television movie. As I remember, I was setting out to detect mismatches among these three sources of information. The lesson learned was to take notice but never rely upon the word of a convicted murderer as a basis.

---

13 Bugliosi, V. & Gentry, C. (1974), *Helter Skelter: The True Story of the Manson Murders*. W. W. Norton & Company, New York, New York, United States. ISBN: 978-0393322231.

This case easily puts Mr. John Q. Public into a position of thinking he can only rely upon the word of a convicted murderer to know what happened and who did what. There is a solution in situations where the basis has to be something other than the only living eyewitnesses and this is the situation in this case. After much thought, the only sound basis would be the physical evidence. This seems to be difficult to comprehend or accept by most people because they are romantically inclined. That is to say, they have come to over-rely on human relations to the exclusion of all else.

    There are several examples of over-reliance on romantic inclinations worth noting in this case. In one instance, the police insisted that it had to be someone who knew the victims at the crime scene. In another later instance, the criminals were not so bad anymore and should be released because they mellowed out. In both of these examples, romanticism got to the point that it clouded judgment.

    Romantic inclination is where nearly everyone goes awry. People get sucked into this case because of its frequent romanticizing. To be clear, the overriding problem with that prevailing attitude is that the only possible eyewitnesses for reconstructing how the murders in this case occurred were the convicts themselves, because everyone else other than the murderers died at the scene of the crime. There remains only one way to acquire a valid basis.

    We also have to reject the one eyewitness who did not actually commit a murder at the scene of the crime. This person is in fact an accessory to first degree murder that got off the hook by turning state's evidence. This eyewitness clearly saw one of the murders being committed. However, even in that one instance where the state granted immunity, the detective has to discriminate. A crime as horrific as murder was not reported to the police by this person, nor was there any attempt to run from the scene even though the opportunities were many. The murderers were directly abetted by this accessory, including handing a weapon to one of the killers during the commission of these crimes as well as disposing of evidence. The next night this person drove the murderers to another slaughter knowing full well what was going on. The conclusion can only be made that there is no person who can act as a basis.

If the comparison is going to be done right in order to determine what exactly occurred, we have to start with a piece of physical evidence and work our way out. That is to say, a fingerprint left at the scene of the crime has to first match to one of the suspects and then be connected to the information gleaned from that suspect. The physical evidence can interrogate the information obtained from the convicted murderers and any of the accessories in order to detect discrepancies. The physical evidence will have to remain the objective basis against which all other interpretation must conform. From this avenue of approach, careful testing of the information from the criminals themselves becomes a somewhat useful if not complex task, because there was more than one murderer involved. It is a good thing to pause and think about how information coming from a convicted murderer should be received, if at all.

More recent examples of overreliance on romanticism are in the exploration of Manson Family members returning to the scene of the crime and tampering with evidence before the police arrived. The basis for exploring the tampered evidence hypothesis is the word of a convicted murderer. Again, the most significant pieces of information about the evidence came to be known by the murderers at the trial. Over time, some tangential questions about the evidence would become weaponized when the convicts sensed their earlier efforts to obfuscate might offer them a potential legal wedge on these minor details. For example, we have a piece of evidence that raises a question and a convicted murderer later learns of this, jumps up, and offers an explanation to add to their continued obfuscation. For most, the word of a convicted murderer is their basis, and therefore, is to be outright rejected.

First, we are looking for information mismatches between the murderers themselves. There are three possibilities: 1) agreement among the murderers 2) apparent mismatches between the murderers, or 3) glaring mismatches between the accounts of the murderers, as in, contradiction. After sorting out the three possibilities, I perceived that the most benefit would come from keying in on the glaring mismatches as part of a process of elimination. It is not necessarily a mismatch if the accounts differ but do not clearly contradict each other, and these can fall into the agreement category or the apparent mismatch category as it becomes clearer where it will fall. The process of elimination will come in two forms: 1) having to toss out contradictions absent further successful information extraction, 2) rejection as to feasibility, as in, one person cannot be in two places at the same time.

Not everyone's account will be exactly identical since it will involve different angles of visibility as to each perpetrator's individual placement during the commission of the crimes. A mosaic of the murderers' accounts is then assembled and mapped to each individual event occurring at the crime scene before attempting to unify event sequencing into one timeline. We are first looking for discrepancy among the murderers as one output, and then discrepancy according to each individual murderer as a set of outputs. The detective then attempts a deconfliction, and where no resolution exists, elimination occurs. The remaining constituent pieces are then collocated as a "known known" mosaic. We are left with a set of "known unknowns", and anything else falls into an "unknown unknowns" category.

A set of question marks will inevitably arise, but they will land in the right places. Agreement might be found for several discreet elements about the crime across all of the accounts. This too will vary among the murderers since the human mind processes something seen to a greater extent than another's. Meaning attaches ever so differently where one person senses some aspect of the same particular event that the other did not, and this will have bearing as to the likelihood that a particular event occurred.

Assigning meaning to observations made by the murderers may also have some bearing in determining with more precision the way a particular event at the crime scene occurred. Likelihood can be quantified according to a Likert scale or some other helpful quantification method that tracks variance as the movement of a previously "known unknown" goes into the "known knowns" category. Unless the force of argument makes it a known, it will become a study of probability, and the final result of that known can only be mathematically stochastic. The categories containing stochastics can achieve best-fit so long as variances are exhaustively accounted for.

As to variances, it is understood that one murderer's mind will focus more sharply on the visual aspect whereas another murderer present has a less visual focus. This kind of variance occurs because visual impression is being attenuated in favor of processing both visual and aural effects in that other murderer's mind. Specifically, one murderer relates visual observation of a punching motion coupled with an audible scream versus another murderer present at the same moment in time relating only that a knife made a stab into a body. One observation is more visually focused than the other's observation, because of how different minds are predisposed to process audio and visual sensory inputs as they occur in the sequence of events. Neither observation is false. Complication by the degree and type of illegal drugs altering normal human audio-visual perception is a confounding variable. Keep in mind that the murderers in this case also had a chance to collaborate afterwards about important details concerning these crimes with the intent of further frustrating the assignment of specific responsibility.

Specific levels of accountability became unachievable early into this case. It should not be forgotten that stories changed when it served the interests of one of the murderers to do so, or the murderers took delight in changing their stories in order to further inflict pain on the affected families. The murderers retained some element of information power in doing so. To complete the emerging timeline, the assembled work would have to be put under the microscope to further prune the information and punish an evasive murderer accordingly. Where the information from this process meets the physical evidence, the physical evidence will always be the determinant.

Any glaring contradictions will stand out. What we can do is determine who among them is withholding a piece of needed information and explain to them why they must know the answer, under threat of negative consequence. We can also ask why one of the murderers did not see what one of the others present saw and apply methods that attempt to extract an answer. Once a unified sequence of events is established by this method of information extraction, a move-by-move timeline will start to emerge. The more events formally established on the timeline by this method, the better the timeline can be set into a more fluid motion that moves any remaining question marks into the right places. The full picture will never emerge due to human limitations on the ability to comprehensively perceive. This particular limiting aspect of human perception will not interfere with securing a conviction. The detective hands these findings to the prosecuting attorney. A careerist type detective would then record his procedure for future study and application.

For instance, we cannot expect the murderers to recall the eye color of the people that they murdered one by one, even though they looked into the eyes of these people. The most we could hope for would be that the murderers noticed perhaps light-colored or dark-colored eyes in this example of perception processing variance. What is left from the entire process can still never become a basis. The basis remains the physical evidence against which the information extracted from the murderers may or may not align. That was the thought process going into the entire comparison effort because books about the crime were overwhelmingly romantically inclined.

Right off, I noticed there were both apparent and glaring contradictions to these accounts during my three-way comparison. The only way to do the comparison was to be able to reenact how the murders went down move-for-move because that is about all one could really do with the preponderance of information provided. I wound up at first with about fifty possible scenarios and eventually ruled out about half of them after this extremely concentrated analysis. The remaining scenarios were insufficient to make a complete enough picture that would draw salient conclusions about who did what in the exact sequence of events. Only a partial animation was possible.

There was a strong desire to get at the truth about what happened for those places in the story that were still missing, because they were crucial to moving forward. The more an unknown is made known, the greater the sense of closure. That is to say, we no longer have to expend energy on "known knowns" by dwelling on them. The reason for prioritizing the expenditure of energy on efforts was to open up the aperture and achieve the most complete picture possible, which would in turn permit seeing and exploring any further interconnections without having to resort to speculation. Detailed work is all-consuming. Any prompt for expanding the scope should only be to reduce the chance of missing the forest for the trees.

Central to this case are particular details about the murder of Sharon Tate since the sworn depositions, testimony, retraction, and backpedaling took place before, during, and after the trial. This was an attempt to frustrate the full measure of justice being brought to bear for Sharon Tate's murder in particular. Obfuscation of the truth is a further offense because this was an obstruction of justice by the accused.

We have bodies all over the place, physical evidence of atrocities committed on their persons, and the system allows the suspects to confess to doing it in such a generalized manner that they are misleading investigators as to who is responsible for exactly what. As it stands, it is a calculated method of deliberately inflicting pain on the families. Not only is it a means of compounding their irresponsible conduct, it is contemptible in the extreme that the system allows them to carry out these types of further offenses. Taking a step back from crime scene analysis after this comparative exercise, I began to seek out the most basic of information about who the murdered persons were. It seems not everyone did likewise because for some reason this aspect was not of interest to people.

    I came to the conclusion back then that there was just going to be little attention to learning about the lives of the persons murdered, even though you could sense that there was some measure of socially desirable prominence to these persons beyond the superficial. The reason for this may or may not have been the desire of the families. In particular, information about Sharon Tate as a person remained vague, even after a dedicated search by all available means.

    For someone like Sharon Tate, people tend to see "movie star" in their mind, pause to review the movies she appeared in, and leave it at that. Movies with Sharon appearing in them either became a way of seeing her likeness when she was still alive, or a morbid form of entertainment for some people who are seeking a means of exploitation. The persons closest to Sharon were so heartbroken that they were overwhelmed, and in a state of distress. Through no fault of the families, suffering the loss of Sharon's life from an act of evil would impede their ability to find words that would communicate what Sharon meant to them and set the record straight for us. Communication would be possible only from the people that knew Sharon best, but even that would ultimately be insufficient since each person in the world has a different set of gifts, talents, and abilities available to apply. There may be complicating factors such as sibling rivalry or parental conflicts involved that surface over time. The ability to organize thoughts about conveying the life of Sharon would be next to impossible for immediate family members when done through a deluge of strong feelings known only to them.

Taking these thoughts into consideration I sensed that in time, Sharon's dignity would be fought for and won. The reality would be different. The public's interest went entirely into a detailed study of the Manson Family who literally stole the show. Courtroom theatrics superseded Sharon's movies in prominence. Manson would ultimately eclipse Sharon, and that is where we are left today. Some people sought to get in on Manson's new role as the ultimate villain by vocally identifying with him or the murderers, making appearances, hurling obscenities, mimicking the Manson Family lifestyle, or conducting themselves in public as pests that looked like a barbaric menace. It must have been a liberating feeling to remove inhibition from their repressed barbarian selves to do so. The technical term for this is uncivilized.

The phenomenon would find its limits. For instance, when at one point members of the Manson Family shaved their heads, not too many public admirers of Manson followed suit. At the same time, as details of the crimes emerged, anything or anyone remotely resembling Manson or the Manson Family showing their face around town were about to take some wrath from the general public. Retribution began once the jury delivered its verdict.

We were all overcome by the flood of journalism, print media, and television coverage that put the focus on everything but Sharon's life. Subsequent movies involving Sharon had little if nothing to do with her real life. This state of affairs is what this campaign plan addresses. At the same time, looking at movies starring Sharon Tate does not sufficiently reveal what kind of person she was in real life. What struck me as odd about this was that the detectives working on this case were in fact focused on learning of Sharon's real life in the immediate aftermath of the crimes, because they decided that the murderers knew Sharon or someone among the victims.

That the murderers knew any of the people killed was ruled out only after their apprehension several months after the crimes. However, I did take note that I now knew more about the murderers than I did about Sharon herself, and that was a bit disturbing about the entire presentation. Sharon was a movie star who was attacked in her home and not much else it seemed. That is the way it came across then, as it generally does now.

One thing that never changed in me after reconstructing events was that I empathized with what the people experienced during the last moments of life as they were murdered. A lot of time has passed since then, but that aspect of the story just stayed with me. In order to find some light in the darkness, I could only guess what each of their lives was actually like before this crime occurred. There was not very much to go on. Time went by.

When the Internet emerged, I would come across by sheer happenstance some of the various news articles, photos, and what-not pertaining to this case that brought it all back, but this time it was different. I was starting to be able to piece together tidbits about Sharon Tate's life. It was like something new or refreshing to learn of, and it had a happy quality about it. People that knew Sharon were now able to communicate through the Internet, come forward and tell an entirely different story. It was a story of Sharon's life, how she came to pursue an acting career, what tickled her most growing up, and what kind of mother she most certainly was. You had to search for it because the public's interest continued to be on the murderers instead of Sharon and her unborn child. The utter disregard for human life by Sharon's murderers as well as the public's new infatuation with the culture of death is barbaric.

Over time, books containing a collection of significant pieces about Sharon Tate's life started to emerge as well, but they were still lopsided in their emphasis on the murders. There was a small sense of resolution, but it became clear from this information that Sharon was a vulnerable person. Sharon was more introverted than one would expect and was much more innocent as a soul, with this vulnerable personality as a detectable outworking. Sharon's introspection is more pronounced from the days of her youth, and then fades somewhat as working in Hollywood enters her life.

Now that a more positive depiction of Sharon's story was becoming better known, I was disgusted to learn that her good nature was frequently preyed upon, violated, and corrupted at many points throughout her life by less than honorable people. As an introspective person, Sharon was pried apart by people who see others as objects for their selfish gratification and amusement. Sharon handled it well, but it was nevertheless a gross violation.

The beauty of an introspective person exudes from them rather than being forced to the surface by the curious. A gentle soul takes comfort in maintaining a sense of shelter, and routinely cherishes times of solitude. The mere thought of this is unimaginable to some people, and it shows in the many crime scene images that people take delight in showing to others. This will become apparent as we get to know Sharon and the situation better. In more ways than one, our society failed Sharon Tate.

At this point it dawned on me to connect the theft of innocence and the enormous harm that it does. Those who are victimized will most likely become like the people who committed the theft of their innocence. This at first appears to be the case with Sharon, but there are indications that she remained determined to subdue inner conflict and preserve what was important. I was reminded of the innocent girl, who in class when prompted says she wants to remain a virgin until married, and is then scolded by her teacher and classmates to the point of tears for having that kind of desire. The damage done in these situations is usually permanent because young people are particularly vulnerable. That kind of situation is a common violation in a culture of death that takes pleasure in devouring innocence. It is of impure motive to bring up such a question by adults who are on the wrong side of the question. They are not "helping" anything as they claim, when confronted.

It is true that these sorts of occurrences happen amongst peers all the time because society allows degradation to occur from major media producers such as Hollywood. For instance, what we used to rightly call a "hang-up" in earlier times is paraded around in public these days as if it were a virtue and it tends to degrade everything it touches. Barbarianism has built-in philosophical camouflage and is easy to adopt, but real civilization takes effort. After what I discovered from this rededicated effort to learn about Sharon as a person who was caught in the middle of a raging counterculture epidemic, I am now thankful to God for Sharon's life, her parents, their family, and how their real life story is managing to see some of the light of day.

I also began to reflect on how this ordeal affected my own life in the past and the way that these people were presented to us over time. It would be an understatement to say that doing a comparative analysis about these crimes was anything less than sickening. Yet it was still all that most people had to work with. It was necessary to become as objective as possible in accepting that reality, go forward from it, and look for the good wherever it might be found. This is the impetus behind designing a campaign plan that brings Sharon's life into proper focus. Hopefully, anyone else going through a similar, objectively based crime scene analysis will themselves come to the same conclusion that now more than ever is the time to act on Sharon's behalf.

Not to act when means exist is an interesting problem in itself. As a citizen, it is appropriate and within your rights to voice concern about some of the past inner workings of Hollywood. There should be not only a Sharon Tate star on the

Hollywood Walk of Fame, there should also be a prominent, public memorial erected that honors her memory in Culver City, California. It is worrisome that our society has been and continues to be on the wrong track if this is going to be the final result for Sharon Tate. This book emphasizes a solution to the problem of human degradation in general, and as it applies to Sharon Tate in particular. Many people really do sense that there is much more potential for good here than first meets the eye. Starting a few years ago I looked for some light in the darkness and believe there is something to say about it.

Sharon Tate from an Original Black and White Image

Photographer Philippe Le Tellier / Paris Match Archive / Getty Images

"Petit a petit, l'oiseau fait son nid"

Artificial Intelligence Colorization of the Original
Sharon Tate Black and White Photo

Photographer Philippe Le Tellier / Paris Match Archive / Getty Images

Introduction

The goal of this book is to present an actionable plan that will reintroduce Sharon Tate to the public, reframe the problem in terms that the public can understand, and explore feasibility at length in order to understand the only way that any Sharon Tate plan would work. Ancillary to that goal is to inform people about Sharon Tate as a person because the public is not really familiar with her life. There is a standalone purpose statement in the next section that leads the reader straight into the main body of the campaign plan. To introduce Sharon Tate in a manner consistent with the outline of this book, there are a few preliminary considerations for the reader to take note.

Sharon worked in the acting profession, amassing an enormous amount of imagery from photographs, television, and movies during her life. Taken together as a visual portfolio, Sharon's media arsenal is a formidable force to be reckoned with should somebody go all out. Not nearly enough work by accomplished professionals that can definitively present Sharon's life in a happier manner occurred since her death, despite the resources to do so.

In the American psyche, Sharon Tate remains increasingly overshadowed by the evermore lurid portrayals of her murder. For me, this alone is enough to cause reflection on the entire situation. The story of Sharon Tate is one of the more striking indications that our society wants to wallow in a culture of death, and Hollywood obliges. After all this, we are still stuck on stupid.

The power of media for good or evil is one of the greatest problems of our time. Media in all of its various forms became a cultural battlespace after robust computerization occurred within our society. There was no corresponding set of active control measures applied to the emerging cyberspace domain that assimilated all manner of media content into its bottomless pit. For lack of foresight, cyberspace was a botched transition that among other things did not have security in mind. This particular security deficiency issue would eventually drive up costs and dilute much of the benefit. There are some other ill effects worth noting as well.

Due to the striation of visual media involved in the case, this is how Sharon Tate as a set of definable problems presents itself to us today. The question is how to proceed. The first order of business would be to reflect on the problem for a while and conduct serious research with further focus on where question marks pop up, as encountered. The next step would be to assemble the research into some kind of logical order, capture and organize the various reflections in one place, and see if and how a narrative would emanate from the collection. This would all be done before initiating a more formalized, deliberative planning process.

If one were to attempt to characterize the entirety of the situation, Sharon Tate probably meets the definition of an "ill-defined problem" or maybe even a "wicked problem." There are ways to tame these ill-defined or wicked problems. Donald Rumsfeld aptly[14] described difficult or super-complex problem resolution in this way: "There are 'known knowns', there are 'known unknowns', and there are 'unknown unknowns.'" That

---

14   Rumsfeld, D. (2011). *Known and Unknown: A Memoir*. Sentinel, New York, New York, United States. ISBN: 978-1595230676.

is a good way to start to think about how we can approach these kinds of problems. I am of the opinion that Sharon Tate is at present an ill-defined problem. This plan intends to at least move the pendulum away from an ill-defined problem status into a steady state or well-defined problem status that campaign plans can greenlight.

One of the first attempts at a more comprehensive Sharon Tate biography for the general public occurred in May of 2000. In Greg King's book – which is at times venerable and at times apologetically exploitative – he mentions[15] that Sharon Tate usually carried with her a copy of Will Durant's book *The Story of Philosophy: The Lives and Opinions of the Greater Philosophers*[16] when she went on long voyages abroad. Durant's brief introduction includes the following philosophical concept that Donald Rumsfeld would later amplify as an approach to the formal planning process: "Philosophy is a hypothetical interpretation of the unknown or of the inexactly known in the front trench in the siege of truth." In addition, books from Sharon's nightstand were up for a November 17, 2018 auction at Julien's in Los Angeles, including her 1957 copy of *The Paradox of Acting* by Dennis Diderot with *Masks or Faces* by William Archer inscribed "Sharon Tate" in Tate's hand (estimate: $800-$1,200).[17]

What we can say from this biographical detail about Sharon is that she was a self-disciplined reader that was well able to navigate substantially abstract and conceptual subjects with a decisively introspective intellect. Images of Sharon seem to almost exude this introspective personality of hers. The question is how we can know Sharon is an introspective person with a

---

15   King, G. (2000). *Sharon Tate and the Manson Murders*. Barricade Books Inc. Fort Lee, New Jersey, United States. ISBN: 978-1569801574.
16   Durant, W. (1961). *The Story of Philosophy: The Lives and Opinions of the Greater Philosophers*. Simon and Schuster, New York, New York, United States. ISBN: 978-1299781481.
17   Julien's Auctions (2017). *Property from the Estate of Sharon Tate*, 8630 Hayden Place, Culver City, California 90232.

higher degree of certainty. There is a clue given to us in a rare 1966 interview of Sharon taken from the interior of the Château de Hautefort where she remarked "The full-time job is to learn your craft and also to try to keep yourself what you really are." We now know from this that Sharon was an actress that drew lines and did not permit the profession to dictate what her core personal values were going to be. Nothing is clearer than Sharon's determination to live life with the weightier matters of honoring her parents, marriage, and the bearing of children taking precedence. Sharon knew what mattered most in life despite pressure from many directions to violate her conscience on matters of ultimate importance.

Philosophical considerations also proved to be a considerable obstacle in Sharon Tate's case. It took years to research and resolve these philosophical propositions and how they affect our society. For instance, Hugh Hefner was not just a publisher that Roman introduced to Sharon. Hefner was the ardent proponent of a unique philosophy that he termed the "Playboy philosophy." Hefner wanted the chance to demonstrate that his philosophy was intellectually superior.

At the same time, Hefner was likeable because he outlined and enforced a situation ethic to accompany this philosophy. He was well-articulated, and possessed a non-threatening public demeanor. However, in a 1966 interview[18] with William F. Buckley Jr., Hefner made it clear that marriage was no longer realistic nor the proper approach to life. Hefner's view of marriage is philosophical humanism because it defines the institution in terms of how human beings misbehave. Hefner would propagate his prophetic view of human existence as a publisher where anything considered illicit by him gets publically challenged using the physiological influence of unleashed eroticism. Let us look at the overall result of the Playboy philosophy with the

---

18   Buckley, W. (1968). *The Jeweler's Eye: A Book of Irresistible Political Reflections*. Putnam, New York, New York, United States. ISBN: 9781111606787.

benefit of hindsight.[19] Hefner's unremarkable contribution to philosophy was in reality a coy play upon the *substantia nigra* part of the brain in humans which signals potential reward as part of its built-in survival instinct. In nearly every sense of the word, Hefner's philosophy driving his view of the world was humanism at its core, and in that respect hardly different than Manson's.

The way that I was able to resolve this seemingly insurmountable obstacle regarding Sharon was to recognize that there were many exotic sounding philosophies going through trial and error during that particular period of cultural upheaval. Society became someone's laboratory or guinea pig to conduct experiments on. What took centuries of constructive effort in order for the United States to emerge as a vibrant constitutional republic appears to be of little value to humanists. In some instances, the deleterious effects of entertaining these new sounding philosophies have not yet completely played out in our society. There is simply no way that Sharon could know what we know today with the benefit of hindsight. At that time, there was a maelstrom of these philosophizing gurus effectively seducing people and carrying out "modern" alternatives upon the unsuspecting.

I came to the conclusion that Sharon was particularly vulnerable, and that Roman had a corrupting influence on her more serious than previously understood.[20] Sharon always held most dear her upbringing and this would prevail in the end. I confess that this was the most difficult area about Sharon's life to resolve which caused a long delay in going forward. What appeared to be permanent damage to Sharon's dignity was

---

19 District Attorney of Dallas County, Appeal from the United States District Court for the Northern District of Texas, No. 70-18. October 11, 1972.
20 King, G. (2000). *Sharon Tate and the Manson Murders*. Barricade Books Inc. Fort Lee, New Jersey, United States. ISBN: 978-1569801574. "Hal Gefsky and Herb Browar were dining at a restaurant in Hollywood when they happened to spot Polanski across the room. Gefsky waved him over, and asked how Sharon was doing. "Oh, Hal," Roman answered, "I've completely corrupted her!" p.85.

exactly what Sharon triumphed against in the last months of her life. I became convinced that telling her story was now an imperative because what was once an uncertainty about her real self was now a known.

The more I researched, the more the unknowns about Sharon Tate became knowns. However, to my own delight I also noticed a happy storyline emerging in the background of a wonderful and old-fashioned gal, in many ways more like her mother Doris than not. Identifying Sharon's indicators and making sure of them took a great deal of effort before I could develop an actionable plan. Let us review for a moment how planning initiation and sustainment occurs in the abstract. The ability to differentiate between the known and unknown with increased fidelity can lead to the development of working assumptions that will allow a given planning process to go forward on a trajectory. Many plans run into the problem of unsound assumptions, insurmountable odds, or situations of looming capitulation. There were more than enough reasons in this case not to capitulate. The feasibility of any given plan would be one determination we could make in light of the knowns.

Also important to understand is that a deliberate planning process would first develop, refine, and then evaluate a set of flexible options. Flexible options make things actionable after a decision authority carefully weighs the merits and demerits of each option. A series of options would in turn be made available to admirers of Sharon Tate and other interested parties in going forward. The second order of business would be to identify how learning of Sharon's life would be in everyone's interest. Sharon is for all intents and purposes a creature of Hollywood, but not what you might think. This working assumption will definitely color the planning process in an unusual direction.

A semi-formal campaign plan touching on all the difficult areas about Sharon Tate's life should inspire others to work at overcoming various problems from every conceivable angle so that the most fitting Sharon Tate commentary is found. The goal here is not to provide arguments to bicker or squabble over with others, but to displace petty quibbling with a headstrong action plan that has enough resilience to stay focused on target throwing the entire culture of death into a tailspin.

This plan is semi-formal only in the sense that it is logically organized. Much of the contemplation within the following pages is a necessary step to begin the process of formalization. Once refined, a great deal of the preliminary discussion presented within this book would eventually become a supporting Appendix to Annex D with a quick reference flowchart. What would then be left is a formal campaign plan.

The knowns would become more certain; some of the "known unknowns" would become knowns. There will likely remain "unknown unknowns", or information that we are unaware about. A formalized campaign plan would help mitigate risk in the area of the "unknown unknowns." We begin with the "known knowns", or things that we know that we know about. From there, several assumptions about the set of knowns will become apparent. For instance, we can assume that Sharon Tate and the American psyche regarding her are, and will continue to be in the public's interest for the foreseeable future. We can also assume that long since entrenched ideological disarray disrupting public policy will continue in ways that frustrate the order of the jury to put Sharon's murderers in front of the executioner, opting instead for parole or death by natural causes such as disease and old age. We can also assume that the culture of death that causes this disarray will not give up power without a fight. These assumptions will serve as a baseline from which all other planning considerations proceed.

A lot of the planning process is hard work. Syntax can have a dramatic effect in key places of the plan requiring a readdress each time an alteration within the plan occurs. The more effort that is put into research, the higher the overall resolution. The set of working assumptions will become more certain. Research intensity will also ensure that we are on the right track in general. The good thing about the formalized planning process is its way of organizing thoughts, its validation by and through inductive, abductive, and deductive processes, the elimination of clutter, and its way of conveying how people can make the most helpful of contributions in going forward. It is important to avoid the temptation to say something about this case that we only wish the case would say. Emphasis should be on what we can say, and continuous attention to how we say it.

For instance, we can say that all unmarried men are bachelors, but we cannot say that a bachelor is at the same time married. There is no other valid interpolation for these frames of reference. Sharon is not the only problem in view in this plan because the murders terrorized the entire country if not the better part of the civilized world. Social justice for Sharon would have to occur on a grand scale. This plan explores and proposes how a scalable structure of social justice might occur for Sharon Tate.

There are few means of communication that are more effective for grand scale endeavors than Hollywood cinema. However, an ephemeral flash in the pan is not envisioned for properly restoring Sharon within the American psyche. However it is that her restoration winds up being accomplished, the ability to shatter Sharon's unhappy enigma in favor of a happier story would certainly benefit from a big budget Hollywood production that achieves a more stable and sustainable trajectory.

Sharon Tate was robbed of her life. Yet since then, a pattern of focusing solely on her murder and an increasingly profane portrayal of human degradation continues to prevail beyond the pale of any civilized society. Part of the problem is found with the propagation of a culture of death that practices degradation as a way of living. Philosophical tradeoff has an allure to it or else people would not fall into its grasp. Media of any form is an instrument for promoting the common good, but the portrayal of social dysfunction as normative has implications. One in five adults in our society suffers a disorder that impairs their ability to recognize reality from make-believe. Based on that statistic, what kind of media ought to be going on cutting room floors to reduce confusing reality with the make-believe, and how else could we go about reversing a reckless if not self-defeating system?

There are probably a number of ways to reverse course that have some manner of validity, but to me, devising a plan of some type is foremost. This publication is the result of a lot of work, and it does the job. The result represents a twenty-thousand foot view from above which navigates through all of the major factors one would typically encounter in traversing Sharon's enigma. Hopefully, the structure of this book causes readers with fresh eyes to think of something helpful as they read along. Subject matter experts can look at this blueprint and forge collaborative efforts for Sharon that focus on a specific area relative to where they are in life. The intent of the plan presented in this book is innocent, and this should become apparent early on for readers. The right resolution to the Sharon Tate question ultimately depends on defining an end state that would better serve the common good.

I am asking for your help.

Michael A. Walker
June 30, 2018

"It is even better to act quickly and err than to hesitate until the time of action is past"

Carl von Clausewitz

A Die Hard Sharon Tate Fan's Memorabilia Display

Used with Permission / All Rights Reserved

Statement of the Purpose

To capture thoughts or reflections in one place about how best to repair and leverage Sharon Tate as an agent for good in the world, inspiring Hollywood as an institution to seek out the dignity and well-being of its full complement of professionals that affects lives in the greater community for the better.

> "Plans are worthless,
> but planning is essential"
>
> *Dwight D. Eisenhower*

Sharon Tate Poses for *Esquire Magazine* January 1, 1967

Photographer William Helburn / Corbis Premium Historical Collection / Getty Images

Rationale

In light of what transpired, has Sharon Tate's dignity remained intact? If her dignity is in question, is it salvageable? As far as her murder is concerned, Sharon lost her dignity because of it, her killers evaded paying the ultimate price, and we are left with a paradox. From every other indication as discussed throughout the following pages, the answer to questions regarding the feasibility of repairing Sharon's dignity is "yes" on all counts. However, there are identifiable problems to overcome. Technically, this would be a qualified yes at this point in time.

Ultimately, the motivation for having a Sharon Tate campaign plan of this type and at this point in history should be to locate Hollywood's latent potential for dramatizing what is good in our world. Of all the Manson murders, Sharon Tate is different in that she was a celebrity. Her status offers rather unique equities for scholars working in the fine arts and social sciences. Over the past few years, researchers, historians, and writers began to ponder the expansive scope of Sharon Tate's life. A carefully delineated investigation into Sharon's life offers all of us hope of a happy resolution, as well as a story brimming with depth.

Sharon Tate is to come under special social protection even if it begins fifty years after her murder. The challenge is akin to someone learning to play the piano starting at fifty years old. In support of this concept, research into Sharon's murder has run its unpleasant course to a culmination point and a scholar's research gap indeed exists. Amateur sleuths and other informal researchers are discovering a wellspring of other data and therein a positive portrayal of Sharon's life becomes feasible, waiting only to be composed by someone. As for the more recent developments pertaining to her case, there now exists a more favorable set of conditions than ever before. Presenting Sharon the right way is not only possible, it would be a timely development influencing the course of events. Sharon's portrayal can be done sympathetically and without a mixed message, given the right kinds of building blocks capable of weathering any perfect storm in the other direction.

In theory, movie producers can tell Sharon's story in a joyful manner that an audience could easily identify with and end it there on a happy note. The emphasis would be on accuracy constrained by the principle of special social protection for any matters that do not contribute to Sharon's dignity. The only other conceivable angle is to imaginatively project into the future what Sharon's life would have been, based upon the last known trajectory of her life.

Sharon Tate is an interesting person upon closer examination. Everyone knows how Sharon was murdered, so it is not helpful to include that kind of portrayal of her in future features and audiences can fill in that blank for themselves if they wish. Nevertheless, people who have no integrity to lose will construct conspiracy theories about the murders as a way of continuing to put the focus on Sharon's death. Let us rediscover her life, and test our own ability to show love properly in the process. Motive should include the understanding that there is no blanket approval statement necessary to such a campaign. Sharon is a unique person who is different from all others.

Documentaries serve only an educational or historical accounting purpose, but cinema is an entirely different matter. It is all too easy for much of Hollywood to yield to the temptation of making a string of second-rate entertainment productions focused solely on exploring the limitless depravity human beings are capable of. Neglecting to confront a virtual onslaught of irresponsible or reckless themes in get-rich-quick cinematic productions is not good because it actually costs more in the long-term and there is an odd kind of guilt by association involved.

Actors are not responsible for this state of affairs, because they have to make a living. The levers of power are beyond the actors themselves even when they are organized into unions. Absent an adequate response in a more cheerful direction, a wretched miasma becomes the new Hollywood standard for no other reason than the system permits it or even favors interests that make the quick money at the expense of everyone else's professional integrity and image. There is still rational capacity for exploring and putting forward a Sharon Tate campaign plan if not to offer insight into improvement in a system that allows financial gain for exploitative forms of entertainment.

It is likely Hollywood's future main effort for portraying the life of Sharon Tate has not been conceptualized this way by those in a position to do something about it, but there are some things interested parties and individuals can do. How would one accomplish something meaningful for Sharon? Finding out the better way to do this for her is what ingenuity is all about. In Sharon's case, the more efficient the problem-solving becomes, the greater the reward.

An epic feature about the life of Sharon that emphasizes her more splendid qualities and ends in a creative resolution would be just one example of a bright path forward. Accomplishing the wholesome presentation of Sharon as a person is not reactionary, selective, or disingenuous. The story of her life without rehashing her death would be due compensation for decades of what is a rather repulsive encoding. If Hollywood's *Hays Code* (sometimes referred to as the Motion Picture Production Code)[21] were still in force, the torrent of misrepresentation surrounding the subject of Sharon Tate that routinely occurs in contemporary cinema would be a direct violation of it.

Sharon's dilemma is not the only problem situation one could conjure up for Hollywood producers to consider, but her life on Earth is an endearing subject for many good-natured or curious persons left wondering or simply unaware. Most of her life's story is left lying dormant in an almost embryonic state of masterpiece playwright development. For some unknown reason, Sharon's off-screen life does not yet seem to interest professional writers as much as her death does. There are plenty of ways to entice writers toward a better way. For instance, the exploration and stitching together of various unearthed and happy details about Sharon as a person would tell what is by all measures, an untold story.

In 1922, a trade association began in Hollywood to attempt self-regulate motion picture production in order to increase investment and reduce the chances of government censorship intervention. The original association was the *Motion Picture Producers and Distributors of America* (MPPDA), and its membership included nearly all of the motion picture companies in Hollywood. The MPPDA's first president was Will Hays. By 1934, increasing pressure within government for intervention into Hollywood's motion picture industry led to publication and enforcement of the *Hays Code*. The Hays Code actually worked in practice, producers and executives liked the code, and it deflected government intervention into motion picture productions at the last minute. Political interest for government censorship intervention waned because the Hays Code gave the impression that Hollywood could effectively self-govern, and the quality of productions took on a favorable complexion. The

---

21 Shurlock, G. (1947). The Motion Picture Production Code. *The Annals of the American Academy of Political and Social Science*, Vol. 254.

concept Will Hays put forth for institutional public relations was one of mature and responsible self-censorship within Hollywood.

Nora Gilbert makes an interesting case for the Hays Code in her book *Better Left Unsaid: Victorian Novels, Hays Code Films, and the Benefits of Censorship*.[22] Censorship as a descriptive noun has connotation that often leads to misunderstanding since the Hays Code was a bulwark against ill-equipped censorship. Yes, stakeholders want censorship despite reckless claims of it inhibiting free expression. For example, we cannot have people running around yelling "fire!" in theaters. The concept Gilbert illustrates in the book is what is important to understand, particularly when cinema promotes a more wholesome form of social well-being. A regulatory agency of self-governance would be fitting to describe how the Hays Code actually worked in practice.

The Hays Code also played a significant role in improving public relations with Hollywood, advancing Hollywood's prominence in the world as a beacon of civilization. Likewise, we could provide special social protection for Sharon Tate because she is a murder victim as well as a Hollywood celebrity. The Motion Picture Association of America (MPAA)[23] system has not quite fit the bill for portraying Sharon Tate over the course of fifty years. This is not an open invitation for people to decide upon either, but an appeal for the most noble subject matter experts to study and deliver a proposal to a recognized decision authority. The outcome of a deliberate production code reimplementation process should not conflict, but honor the glorious history and traditions of Hollywood. If we cannot get Sharon Tate right in what comes out of Hollywood, then one flexible option is to reinstate the Hays Code verbatim until the

---

22 Gilbert, N. (2013). *Better Left Unsaid: Victorian Novels, Hays Code Films, and the Benefits of Censorship.* Stanford Law Books, Redwood City, California, United States. ISBN: 978-0804784207.

23 Burroughs, J. (1971). X Plus 2: The MPAA Classification System During its First Two Years. *Journal of the University Film Association*, Vol. 23*(2)*.

situation reverses. A second flexible option is to have even and odd years that Hollywood enforces the Hays Code.

In the bigger picture, there should also be some kind of mechanism that allows for wisdom to distinctively grace the shaping of Hollywood's overall tone regarding Sharon because her acting work was international. As for the American public, big-budget movie productions with the greatest audience reach should set the highest of standards as a matter of principle. Those standards should include the hard cases like Sharon's: Stories that are ingrained in the American psyche, yet provide little information about the subject's personality. Public trust is engendered when the cinematic industry consistently pursues excellence over time. Excellence, as it always has done, it serves as an example to aspiring but serious professionals seeking to work in a complex field.

Hollywood as an institution faced a remarkably similar situation as early as 1927. Back then, motion picture companies remained perplexed by a trend of public discontent with Hollywood's biggest productions. The honorable efforts of Will Hays restored public confidence in Hollywood as its trusted agent. The Motion Picture Production Code of 1930 was a remarkable achievement, but when Eric Johnston replaced Will H. Hays, a drift began in 1956 leading to the blacklisting phenomenon. Amendments to the Hays Code beginning in 1956 quickly led to a collapse of producer confidence in the institution. In 1968, the passive Motion Picture Association of America (MPAA) rating system emerged in which viewers decide based on the given rating. Before the MPAA, the Hays Code buffered the movie industry from outright government censorship but its enforcement became problematic by 1960. Ever more certain of trying something new, Eric Johnston would not consider reassertion of the old Hays Code. The only reason to undermine the Hays Code was because of its effectiveness. There is a good case to be made that the current situation is different because it is driven in part by a society that has now come to expect negativism to prevail as a theme in entertainment.

It is important to understand subsequent fragmentation of the production code beginning in 1957 as it relates to Sharon Tate. The undeniable lack of active measures present in the 1968 MPAA system did little to halt a crescendo of negativism and the advocacy of divisive causes in cinema, forming an increasingly counterproductive spiral. The enticing proposition was that we are to explore the full-orbed human experience in cinema, but this plan takes the position that it is not good or necessary to hang out the dirty laundry. Most people want to be at peace, knowing what the boundaries are, and not be conditioned to tolerate something known to be repulsive about humanity. Conditioning causes society to consider something that is depraved and that in itself is a theft of innocence. To expose this means of exploitation is a flexible option in this campaign plan.

In hindsight, the MPAA approach is anything goes, but it gives movies a rating intended to stagger viewership for those individuals who adhere to MPAA ratings as a decision rule for what to watch. The problem is that the MPAA system appears to lack the ability to retain the respect of viewing audiences over time. Even if the culture were given over to wickedness, Hollywood would have the capacity to be a light in that darkness through the reimplementation and enforcement of active measures straight out of the Hays Code.

Some producers want to tinker with the lines between the MPAA ratings out of disrespect for that system. This is called "progress" in order to conceal what is a further theft of innocence through exploitative conditioning. It is no surprise that this mindset reels in horror at the thought of the Hays Code being reinstated, because the producers would never get away with ignoring the rules. In the past, if a producer put a movie up for release authorization that was in clear violation of the Hays Code, the makers would have to either edit it or wind up selling it overseas, but either way it was going to cost millions of dollars. When the MPAA came along, the effective checks and balances of the Hays Code were formally relaxed. There was no resulting progress.

By way of contrast, the system of professional sports in the United States like boxing, football leagues, or Major League Baseball is part of an institution in society that has managed to maintain its own set of active measures. Professional sports have a clearly defined set of "unsportsmanlike conduct" rules which tends to engender the public's trust. Unsportsmanlike conduct infractions are dealt with on the spot. Movie producers get to commit unsportsmanlike fouls all over the place and in today's Hollywood they just receive a rating for it. Hollywood is in need of a system of penalty enforcement.

The end state of a smartly devised Sharon Tate campaign could be defined as the re-emergence or new dawn of Hollywood's golden era that embraces the aim of increased public trust. This is a bit vague as to providing an adequate rationale, but realistically it would be like an epiphany of sorts and not so much a discreet point. There would likely have to be a convergence of several forces that resembles how the golden era of Hollywood emerged in the past. The story of Sharon Tate's life converging with Hollywood at some point would without a doubt become a defining moment.

The procedure for moving forward would have to be considered in a way that firmly secures the end state, and a specific campaign plan such as Sharon Tate's is a good place to start. At present, Sharon Tate not only remains an ill-defined problem, but is oftentimes beset with completely unrelated interests claiming her as their own. The ensuing chaos tends to set people at odds with one another. At a bare minimum, an attempt to reconstruct Sharon Tate for good purposes could serve as a test case, or a proof of concept. A determined effort aimed at defeating the prevailing attitude toward Sharon's life might serve as a beacon for envisioning Hollywood's old glory days brought to life. What is good about life can find itself once again in Hollywood after surviving the storms of the past. The Hays Code can and should make an intrusion into the present.

Like other institutions in society, the cinematic enterprise concentrated in Hollywood can work to protect its actors' dignity in difficult but manageable cases. We destroy the scourge of the Manson Family and society's fixation with their barbarism by ignoring them and promoting Sharon Tate optics instead. Sharon Tate can creatively fit into the eternal story of good triumphing over evil, which is a time-tested formula that Hollywood has been known to work spectacularly well with in the past. In the development of this rationale, we see two divisions of a main effort. The first effort is to ignore barbarism as well as the philosophical foundations that encourage it. The second effort is to exact a displacement of Manson with Sharon Tate so that the two are no longer linked in the American psyche. The outlook for this rationale is without a doubt challenging.

Hollywood's ultimate weapon from Sharon's arsenal is her dazzling, photogenic appearance. Add to that a wholesome understanding of her as a wonderful old-fashioned gal who was raised right, and you have the right chemistry. There is simplicity yet enormous potential when objective and subjective forms of beauty converge. Solving the problem of how to leverage Sharon Tate's optics to maximum effect in modern times presents a challenge to future producers. If in agreement that Sharon Tate was already an actress in multiple starring roles, then a case could be made that she was on the verge of a breakthrough into superstardom. It would make for an excellent fictional portrayal, based on that reality, just how Sharon would have actually accomplished superstardom given her real-life trajectory when she died. It should be agreeable to everyone that Sharon was at least considered a potential contender in the superstardom lottery at the time of her death. This would be a flexible option for writers and movie producers to consider.

On the surface it seems impossible to accomplish decisive resolution given the current Sharon Tate situation. Her murderers seek release at every opportunity as they grow old or happen to die from natural causes. Spurred on by a legal system suffering from years of having the wrong people in power, the new normal is going to wind up being a mockery of legal justice in Sharon's case. Social justice for Sharon – however long it may be in coming – should be exacted in such a way that she is made adorable as a person and ultimately overpowering to audiences. Sharon Tate at present is an unhappy enigma.

This rationale is not centered on the actions of individuals alone. A strategy that prompts movie industry representatives to exercise a test bed of active controls applied to movies about Sharon – in phases if necessary – would help everyone to organize thoughts around her case as an act of special social protection. When it comes to Sharon Tate, degradation of any form is forbidden. Planning could address in detail how to go about prompting corporate moviemaking decision-makers to take a second look at the Sharon Tate problem and act with a higher degree of certainty or clarity on this matter. Sharon's allies should be able to better see where and how the many talented individuals available could begin to tackle the problem at all sorts of levels. For example, a good book makes a great screenplay, and so forth.

Writers could apply their energies by employing the finest of writing skills that would contribute to a more well-defined end state for both Sharon Tate and Hollywood together as one. A secondary goal or effect would be to seek, find, and resolve specific problem areas enough to rectify what turned out to be a wrongdoing in Sharon's case. Planners can group problem areas into a rank-ordered list and strategize from an analysis of each area's strengths, weaknesses, opportunities, and threats. For the top five threats or weaknesses internal and external to Sharon Tate, this plan takes the position that in those most dicey of areas, Sharon is to be protected from reproach as a murder victim.

People that advocate or otherwise idolize Manson Family murderers can be identified and monitored by the authorities in a sweeping move to suppress under domestic terrorism laws overseen by the Department of Homeland Security. If Manson has stolen Sharon's celebrity, then Homeland Security can blacklist Manson Family murder advocates for monitoring on that basis. Constituents can write their representatives to request the allocation of more funding for this purpose along with dedicated university research grants that study this particular criminal phenomenon as a significant domestic concern that also has international implications. Hollywood movie production corporations can point to official sanctions against Manson murder advocates in order to blacklist the more recalcitrant movie producers as a show of support for the authorities. For years, surviving family members of the Manson murders were put in the position of having to confront those few who would exploit Sharon's death in the movie and music industries.

We often hear the expression "building a culture of life" but after realizing that this would indeed be a noble thing to do, we are pretty much left dumbfounded. Most people would not know how to go about doing it because with little exception we have lost sight of what right looks like anymore. Part of the reason for this is that negativism as an outlook is always easy to adopt and propagate. Negativism as a way of life is indeed the natural tendency and therefore the domain of the slothful. This trend toward a prevailing mood of negativism has led to topsy-turvy applications regarding real life concerns.

For example, a reasonable level of modesty, even when done with the most splendid elegance, is almost reviled even though it is the superior form. Questionable persons see any attention to modesty as something to be rejected or openly ridiculed. This zero tolerance attitude seems irrational because excessive immodesty is almost always a distraction. It is as if producers are actually hiding something by being intentionally immodest. The human imagination is easily given to impression, and visual media can suffer from a kind of malpractice. It is no wonder we seem to punish any attempt to grow the culture that produces the Shakespeares of our time, because constructive effort takes serious work.

Sharon Tate gives us a glimpse at how we could go about planning her encore style introduction to the American public. There is sufficient and compelling rationale to go forward with the development of a campaign plan that would actually measure performance, allowing us to glimpse future horizons. As if her death was not bad enough, Sharon was systematically robbed of her celebrity. There is a way to measure the Sharon Tate differential with a forecast based on her last known trajectory. People from all sorts of backgrounds would likely be able to see the benefit and shared interest in a plan that ignores Manson, and promotes Sharon Tate.

"By beauty I mean that quality or those qualities in bodies by which they cause love or some passion similar to it"

Edmund Burke

Photographer Bill Ray / The LIFE Picture Collection / Getty Images

Assessment

Given the considerations outlined in the rationale for a campaign plan as ambitious as this one, it can be done. Media of all kinds in the right hands is a powerful enough instrument to accomplish the larger objectives, and we do have the raw materials to work with in Sharon's case. Aside from her murder, Sharon Tate is no Humpty-Dumpty, and neither is Hollywood. Hindsight is 20/20 when it comes to Sharon's death, but her life? Not so much – at least not up until this point in time. In order to render an honorable movie portrayal of Sharon Tate's real life, writers are going to have to make an assessment of her personality.

In working on an assessment of Sharon Tate's personality, the researcher becomes aware of a significant transition occurring within the last year of her life. There are continuities and discontinuities but we cannot know if her transition would be a permanent change of temperament because she died. Sharon became pregnant, and up until then exhibited an adventurous personality most evident in her cataloging of experiences. Sharon quickly became more intuitive and judging but remained introspective throughout this transition. The causes of the transition are many but it is not far from the truth that Sharon was raised a certain way that allowed her to draw upon this foundational experience. Sharon's self-respect came into conflict with the life she felt she was living to the point that Sharon went with what she intuitively knew. The first major assessment of Sharon Tate's personality is that there was a rapid and significant personality shift occurring just before her death.

There are a lot of indicators one could attempt to attribute to a given personality category, but several indications stood out more loudly than others on a first pass at studying Sharon Tate's personality. For instance, the founder of Filmways Martin Ransohoff assessed Sharon Tate at first as lacking confidence in front of television show cameras and in need of exposure to overcome this. Ransohoff's professional judgment about Sharon is one indicator of her introspective personality. Indicators from subject matter experts weigh heavily in personality assessments. The vetted and assigned weights to personality profiles are useful to potential screenplay writers.

For the major personality traits, Sharon continued to exhibit openness and agreeableness more than conscientiousness and neuroticism. In the big picture, Sharon grew weary of a somewhat peripatetic existence, indicated by her desire to settle down and raise a family with a greater sense of stability. The reasons for adopting this indicator in a personality assessment are Sharon's previous cataloguing of experiences behaviorism, beginning with her first acting role in the movie *Barabbas*, quickly followed by Sharon seeking special permission (due to her age) in order to make a trip from Italy to Hollywood.[24] Sharon was going to attempt an acting career that would take her on a carousel of movie sets.

What we can say from this rapid series of events is that Sharon was at least decisive about what kind of work she wanted to do for a career. A supporting indicator would be for the researcher

---

24 King, G. (2000). *Sharon Tate and the Manson Murders*. Barricade Books Inc. Fort Lee, New Jersey, United States. ISBN: 978-1569801574.

to take notice that Sharon rarely wore the same set of clothes twice, but this was not out of her dissatisfaction with the outfits. Sharon was cataloguing experiences by donning a linear but ever increasing wardrobe inventory. This pattern continued until the last six months of her life where Sharon definitely wanted to settle down in a home and indicated displeasure at going home alone in order to give birth.[25] The assessment for this indicator is that Sharon Tate's need for a cataloging of experiences was sufficient by that point in her life, signaling a personality transition.

The most striking example of Sharon remaining introspective throughout this transition is her strong inclination to live in a secluded house that she started moving into on February 14, 1969.[26] The house that Sharon liked was also at the end of a road, perhaps likeable to her because it would reduce traffic volume and offer a sense of peace from increasingly unsettling commotion. Sharon's portfolio of experiences as a personality characteristic quickly turned into her becoming the architect of a fledgling family. This personality shift was not Sharon merely reinventing the wheel. This time it was going to be Sharon's own family and it is conceivable that stability would be something excitingly new to her because she moved around a lot growing up. At around the same time, Sharon's father was retiring from his career and her family was already in the process of moving nearby which would provide an extra sense of stability. What we can say about this assessment is that Sharon underwent a change in priorities, and this plan takes the position from that assessment that Sharon selected the right priorities based on her upbringing.

Another indication of Sharon's personality transition is how she started showing signs indicating she was growing

---

25   King, G. (2000). *Sharon Tate and the Manson Murders*. Barricade Books Inc. Fort Lee, New Jersey, United States. ISBN: 978-1569801574.
26   Bugliosi, V. & Gentry, C. (1974), *Helter Skelter: The True Story of the Manson Murders*. W. W. Norton & Company, New York, New York, United States. ISBN: 978-0393322231.

weary of living like chaff in the wind between Europe and the United States. She was at the new house for about a month, back overseas for about four months, and then back home for a little over two weeks before she died. That means Sharon was physically present at her new, yet secluded residence for a total of only 59 out of 176 days, or 8 of 26 weeks. It is likely Sharon's reason for going through with *The Thirteen Chairs*[27] movie is because she had star billing, it paid her over a million in today's dollars for about a month's work, she would have a chance to see her husband nearby, and the production could effectively work around her pregnancy with resequencing techniques. Sharon stayed on in London, England for the entire month of May, June, and half of July. Despite pressure to deliver her baby in Europe, Sharon had enough of it and went home. She was becoming less agreeable and perhaps more competitive because her performance in *The Thirteen Chairs* was arguably her most confident.

Sharon had numerous dogs as pets but her herding of stray cats suggested she began to fill up empty places and unmet needs with closeness to these creatures beyond simple companionship. The explanation for this is found in the recent loss of one of her dogs[28] and an increasing level of disappointment with people that Sharon overly trusted. Sharon was still happy to be who she was because she maintained her self-respect throughout ongoing challenges with people around her. Apparently, Sharon's previous catalog of experiences in learning of the world was behind her. In addition, Sharon's mom, Doris Tate, brought Sharon the wooden rocking chair used by Doris and Doris's mom to rock newborns with. What we can say about these developments is that Sharon became more attracted to thoughts of a brighter future than the here and now emphasis she displayed in the past. The assessment for this mapping is

---

27 Compagnia Generale Finanziaria Cinematografica (1969). *The Thirteen Chairs*. IMDb title tt0065361.
28 King, G. (2000). *Sharon Tate and the Manson Murders*. Barricade Books Inc. Fort Lee, New Jersey, United States. ISBN: 978-1569801574.

that a significant personality transition occurred within Sharon, with striking indications of rapid gains toward maturity rather than away.

Personality profiles are theoretical and can only achieve a best fit for researchers. There is no hard and fast rule for what indicators to use for an assessment of someone's personality, but what we are looking for is a consensus about a given personality indicator among many that stands out as a marker. Markers are helpful when arranging timelines to study the impact of events upon someone's personality. Personality profile development is qualitative in nature, but over a span of time it can resemble working with a sieve. Personality markers are helpful for assessments. Writers can use Sharon's personality sketch presented here to build a more robust set of Sharon Tate personality guidelines for screenplays.

It would likely take several months of a unified visual and narrative focused effort to see measurable results in a shift of screenplay writing or cinema before public perception of Sharon and Hollywood changes from its current negativistic outlook into a happier storytelling. The implications of having a happy, positive Sharon Tate campaign with all sorts of professionals working on this problem are exciting. It would be interesting to see what creative professionals come up with. The movie could be nostalgic, retro focused, or even the internal workings of Hollywood itself driven by moviemaking professionals of all types working on how to present Sharon's life with the idea that Hollywood does not leave anyone behind on the battlefield. Reintroduction of Sharon to the public can and should occur. For the purpose of realistically assessing this situation, the cost to benefit ratio of reintroducing Sharon is favorable to society in the long term, but the path to implementation remains unknown at present.

Hollywood higher ups could relinquish the appearance of indifference, set a more hopeful tone for the future, and influence efforts in the near term to reach down and pull Sharon up.

Doing that would send a powerful message that crime against a Hollywood professional does not pay. Public awareness working in concert with more wholesome movies focused on the life of Sharon Tate is a goldmine of untapped wealth creation. Sharon was and is entertaining, but we reinterpret wealth here as an abundance of something good. There are uniform ways to measure the course of events related to Sharon Tate in the past, track the present situation, and make a projection into the future that yields a wealth creation estimate.

One metric is the number of movie productions dedicated to telling only the story of Sharon's life versus the number of movie productions rehashing Sharon's death. We can take a closer look at how this metric would have to be set up in order to measure in a way that it tells us something. There are four possibilities for a Sharon Tate screenplay focus: 1) Sharon's life, 2) Sharon's life and death together, 3) Sharon's death, 4) Sharon's future had she lived. Any production that couples Sharon's life and death together would fall into the *steady state* category.

The same metric applies to Sharon Tate book writers. The most difficult quantification would be measuring books or productions that touch on Sharon's life and death together because this would vary as to the degree of one or the other. Books or productions which include references to Sharon's death however varying the proportion might be would indicate the steady state's volatility. We can now track movement.

If a virtual army of genuinely gifted writers were to get at the essence of the Sharon Tate concept upon which this campaign plan builds, then books and screenplays written only about Sharon Tate's life could be measured as a metric against those who want to revisit her death. There may be a way to present Sharon in a book that at the very end briefly states that Sharon's life was cut short, without going into detail. The story of Sharon's life all the way up until but not including her death contributes in the most positive way to society if it can overcome the half century of fascination with her death.

The ability to measure things is enormously helpful to identify the best case for Sharon Tate. It will become necessary to produce the kind of quality that captures the collective imagination of the elite to ensure the loftiest of campaign objectives. Roman Polański will have to be left out of the picture as detrimental. There should be no hidden agenda or baggage attached to the plan and absolutely no ulterior motives involved. An all-out campaign to have a presentable Sharon Tate ready that lacks yesteryear's deficiencies is essential to any effort, large or small.

Despite journalism's fixation on the Manson Family for decades, there is still more Sharon Tate cinematic or raw image media available due to the sheer volume of her visual portfolio. This voluminous body of work created by moviemakers, as well as her personal photographer, represents a fixed number the extent of which is presently not known. Sharon's personal photographer died in November of 2017 and there may be yet unreleased material becoming available in the near future. Never before seen candid images of Sharon are surfacing as well that open up new possibilities. The preponderance of this captured media-rich content occurred in both the movie studio and on location in Italy, Aquitaine, England, and the United States.

There is also historical value appearing within many of Sharon Tate's images that can intensify public interest or provide for the basis of happier messaging. Sharon Tate's visual portfolio is chock full of positive, endearing subject matter. Despite these resources, Sharon's story has not yet been told in a way such that it alters the American perception of her in a happier direction.

The most historic imagery of Sharon Tate is taken from film shoots and stills at the Château de Hautefort in Aquitaine. This massive 17th century "Sun King Louis XIV" period château was just completing a decades-long renovation in 1965 during the filming of *Eye of the Devil*.[29] The fairytale-looking structure is

---

29   Filmways Pictures (1966). *Eye of the Devil*. IMDb title tt0061634.

breathtaking, built on a prominent plateau overlooking a steep hillside that lands in a quiet French country village on one side and a vast winegrowing valley on the other. Château de Hautefort is considered the "Jewel of the Périgord." Although shot in black and white film and never colorized to date, the cinematography of Sharon Tate in this movie is certainly the finest of her career. What makes images of Sharon historically valuable in this instance is that most of the interior of the château burned to the ground – minus its immense stonework – only two years after filming completed. Nearly all the damage to the interior from this devastating fire has since undergone full restoration.

Learning the story of Sharon's life brings joy to people's lives, but there are a few forces at work against accomplishing the objective of an epic Sharon Tate life screenplay. These forces are either internal or external to her. For fifty years, society has voted in favor of a detailed study of the Manson Family at Sharon Tate's expense. There are several explanations for this situation worth exploring and assessing for the purpose of facilitating campaign mobilization.

First of all, there is no valid explanation for Sharon's murder other than at its core it was an irrational act, which is a strong indication of the presence of evil. Yet we have explored evil in the decades since then despite its irrational basis as if it were worthy of serious philosophical consideration or deserving of emulation in a pluralistic society. The weakness of pluralism is in its seeming schizophrenia and public confusion that people often attempt to exploit. In order to take advantage of the weak-minded in this case, some people went so far as to question Helter Skelter as Manson's motive as if voicing doubt vindicates those found guilty of murder. This is a great example of how the culture of death operates. There was no mistrial, and murder is utterly evil. When motive is not necessary to obtain a murder conviction, there is no argument.

The public would benefit from penalizing or removing the more dangerous elements in society who openly advocate homicidal choice. Without realizing it, people of that particular time period were practically embracing a culture of death as their friend, oblivious to the known negative effects of marching down that path in humankind's past. The youth claimed to know things better in those days and there was often an exploitation of that generational divide for less than honorable purposes. Manson attained an odd form of celebrity status as a result of this disarray.

Here we can pinpoint a specific Sharon Tate campaign plan goal starting with a question: What defines the expression "glory days of Hollywood", "Old Hollywood", or "Hollywood's golden era"? The answer to this kind of question is indeed difficult to articulate, but everyone seems to know what you are talking about when referring to that period. For lack of a better explanation, it is a kind of happiness in people being lifted to new heights by Hollywood. There was at one time a simplicity and joyfulness to life in general. It is splendid how old Hollywood captured this sense of joyfulness in its movies, and how that aspect gave motion pictures from the era a timeless feel. A new dawn of Hollywood's old glory days is a worthy goal that Sharon Tate somehow plays a starring role in. The idea is that the initial impetus for having a new dawn depends upon and occurs at the point of a retelling of Sharon Tate's life in an honorable fashion. A new dawn for Hollywood is entirely feasible because it worked before under similar circumstances.

The Hollywood plan presented here is not all that different from how it was in the 1920s era. Wholesomeness and well-being presented by Hollywood's cinematic productions were infectious to the entire world. Without a doubt, Hollywood changed the world for the better. We can track how and where that positive tone began to show a shift away from its seemingly all too fleeting existence.

For one thing, there are too many choices for people these days to the point that it is stressful and oftentimes counterproductive to the attainment of real satisfaction within our society. Everything seems complex whereas before, simplicity was divine. This excessively complex condition contributes to disunity and a large part of that disunity comes from extreme individualism. For instance, when the 9/11 terrorist attacks occurred, the country unified for a brief moment. Do we need terrorism to unify us, or can Hollywood defeat terrorism by unifying us in better ways than it is currently doing? Expert analysis can lead to the development and implementation of a simpler yet effective set of cinematic countermeasures given the lessons learned from the entirety of the American experience. The Hays Code is timeless and helped sanctify Hollywood in a profound way, ensuring its place as a respected institution in society if not the entire world. Never before had an advanced form of civilization reached such heights. The MPAA rating system just gives a finished product a rating on a scale. Verbatim Hays Code reimplementation is a movement whose time has come.

Sharon, like any other normal human being, made silly mistakes in life that some people could not look past upon a superficial examination of her right after the murder. Journalism, either intentionally or unintentionally, confused her real life with make-believe acting work that had the effect of imparting real life blame to her account. The common thread implicit to this journalistic theme was that Sharon created the conditions that led to her murder. The time that the authorities took to track down and apprehend those responsible for her murder only exacerbated this journalistic speculation problem. Again, the historical time period in which the murders took place remains the confounding variable. Further explanation for some of Sharon's life is warranted.

Part of any explanation for the uniqueness of Sharon's life is that she came under pressure to conform to a general breakdown in inhibitions. These pressures were coming from all sorts of different directions characteristic of the period, particularly in the moviemaking field. Sharon felt free and loved to laugh in this time, but soon began to experience the nettles of

ASSESSMENT | 97

internal conflict. However, Sharon was about to deal with those brewing conflicts head on. Her pregnancy settled things down and Sharon was at her most confident point ever in life.

Sharon was starting to conquer the challenges of life, ever learning and drawing upon the well of resources that her upbringing gave her. Needless to say, it was unquestionably a time marked by anything goes experimentation without a corresponding set of brakes to go along with it. Sharon was setting limits as she learned and grew but at the same time she remained trend-setting in her role as a model and an actress. Sharon makes for an interesting study in continuities and discontinuities. It is Sharon who is the perfect storm.

Hollywood movies and television showed the superficialities of that period by visually integrating the new fashions and styles into its productions and programming.[30] Productions also began to delve into the emergent mindset, but the result was an increased frequency of broadcast standards infraction. Not all aspects of the cultural upheaval were so problematic for Hollywood productions, and Sharon falls into this category beginning with her first television role as a recurring character in *The Beverly Hillbillies*[31] and bit parts in the *Mister Ed*[32] show.

As to Sharon Tate's intellectual development, the substance of any claim hinges on the rigor of the academic training that Filmways had Sharon go through. Sharon graduated high school and did about three years of intense academic study in the fine arts. Filmways programmed and oversaw Sharon's demanding regimen.[33] This would be about the equivalent of a bachelor's degree in the liberal arts because her special training was a formalized program of instruction. Sharon completed her Filmways training at the age of 22, so she would

---

30   Cartwright, A. (2014). *Styling the Stars: Lost Treasures from the Twentieth Century Fox Archive*. Insight Editions. ISBN: 978-1608872572.
31   Filmways Television (1963). *The Beverly Hillbillies*. IMDb title tt0055662.
32   Filmways Television (1964). *Mister Ed*. IMDb title tt0054557.
33   King, G. (2000). *Sharon Tate and the Manson Murders*. Barricade Books Inc. Fort Lee, New Jersey, United States. ISBN: 978-1569801574.

fall into the category of an accelerated collegiate equivalence in a standardized academic progress timeline, based on a peer comparison by age in the universal cohort. Evidence in support of this claim is Sharon's continued academic interests beyond training. Sharon read of her own volition an assortment of highly intellectual books that her intense Filmways training no doubt had a considerable influence. In addition, Sharon avidly studied child-bearing books from a self-starting, intellectually curious predisposition. The assessment is that in addition to maintaining a professional career, Sharon Tate held considerable academic aptitude and an equivalency record of achievement at the time of her murder.

Somewhere between the television roles and the later movie roles between 1964 and 1965, Sharon's agent wound up typecasting Sharon into an aesthetic yet tawdry character mold. Exploring this further, it is noteworthy that in 1964, Sharon auditioned for a starring role as Liesl in the film *The Sound of Music*.[34] However, Sharon was deemed not young-enough looking for that role. At first considered "out of fashion" by Hollywood elites, *The Sound of Music* turned out to be the highest grossing film in world history, it held that distinction for the next five years, it retains fifth place for all time to this day, and is arguably the last palpable example of Hollywood's golden days. It is certain that Sharon's agent was under pressure to fulfill the Filmways corporation contract requirements, as part of the Filmways executive director's plan to recoup a return on investment for Sharon's training.

Filmways initially invested nearly one million in today's dollars[35] for training Sharon Tate, and it was a sunk cost. To deal with the situation, Filmway's executive director made the decision to send Sharon to Aquitaine in an immediately available role which would become the 1965 *Eye of the Devil* movie. From

---

34 Robert Wise Productions (1965). *The Sound of Music*. IMDb title tt0059742.
35 King, G. (2000). *Sharon Tate and the Manson Murders*. Barricade Books Inc. Fort Lee, New Jersey, United States. ISBN: 978-1569801574.

then on Sharon seemed typecast in subsequent starring roles for big budget movies, however tawdry the characters she played might be. Not being picked up for *The Sound of Music* production due to her mature appearance was no fault of Sharon's, and this alternative route was the best possible obligation fulfillment for her at that given moment. Sharon arrived in Aquitaine to begin filming. Overseas film productions were under a different set of guidelines than Hollywood.

Hollywood's Hays Code and later the MPAA rating system forced the producer's creative idea generator to overcome situations that came into conflict with both sets of guidelines. Yet producers often managed to achieve rather unexpected, happy results given the constraints. For instance, Barbara Eden's belly button presented a broadcast standards dilemma that the *I Dream of Jeannie*[36] producers grappled with.[37] Regardless of which demarcation point about the Barbara Eden belly-button question one were to take, there is no denying that all sides were at least tickled in part by the lighthearted discussion that it generated. One thing contemporary productions tend to forget in their overreliance on explicitness is that the human imagination is powerful. Except for the most extreme of cases, immodesty is actually a cover-up done to distract an audience from inferior cinematic craftsmanship. Well-done modesty is a fine art. Accordingly, excessive immodesty is just as inferior as excessive modesty, and professionals look for that fine line.

Sometimes producers take unnecessary risks and get caught. One of Sharon's movies, *Valley of the Dolls*,[38] condemned by the autonomous catholic *League for Decency* in 1967 was one of four[39] such condemned films that year. This is a potential problem area for preserving Sharon's dignity as a person. The

---

36   Screen Gems Television (1965). *I Dream of Jeannie*. IMDb title tt0058815.
37   Eden, B. & Leigh, W. (2011). *Jeannie Out of the Bottle*. Crown Archetype. New York, New York, United States. ISBN: 978-0307886965.
38   Red Lion (1967). *Valley of the Dolls*. IMDb title tt0062430.
39   Canby, V. (October 13, 1967). *Filmmakers Show Less Fear of Catholic Office*. New York Times, New York, New York, United States.

assessment is that Sharon had no foreknowledge that this was coming, but the producers did. As for Sharon in real life, she was without question a faithful spouse and sometimes the movie characters she played were not.

The remaining issue is then Sharon agreeing to play such roles after reading the scripts. The assessment for this particular issue is that Sharon was more interested in working with the many famous actresses hired on to *Valley of the Dolls* such as Judy Garland. Sharon was probably relieved if not flattered that she was approached for a starring role in another big budget Hollywood film. Sharon's compelling interest therefore seemed to be at least for the purpose of résumé-building and professional networking, even though Garland was eventually fired from the cast. Here we see the striking difference for Sharon between make-believe and real life.

Sharon's make-believe character in the movie is Jennifer North, whose heart became darkened and murders her unborn child in an abortion. However, in real life, Sharon Tate is quite the opposite. The assessment is that Sharon was a starlet on the rise, so accepting the *Valley of the Dolls* script for acting out this kind of character put her into a calculated risk position. Sharon agreeing to play the part is not to be confused with it being a gesture of approval, but the producers are squarely to blame in this instance. The general public is not completely aware of what actors have to deal with in their profession.

This make-believe versus real life example taken from Sharon's character in the 1967 movie *Valley of the Dolls* compared to Sharon's real self in 1969 is a splendid example of how Sharon is worthy of our admiration as a person. This particular comparison adequately demonstrates how Sharon's human dignity can be defended if not outright proclaimed. If Hays Code enforcement in 1967 actually occurred, it is certain that it would protect Sharon from risqué exploitation by movie production companies, as well as limit unnecessary risk taking by any of Hollywood's actors.

The Motion Picture Production Code and MPAA are a potential complication as they apply to Sharon Tate. Several of her movie parts were foreign productions outside of Hollywood's oversight. However, these foreign movies that Sharon played roles in actually turned out to be of higher standards regarding explicitness. Sharon appears briefly in her first ever movie role in *Barabbas*,[40] a colorful 1961 epic produced in Italy that explores characters central to the Christian faith. The positive reaction to Sharon Tate's small acting role by *Barabbas's* starring actors such as Anthony Quinn and Ernest Borgnine is what led to Sharon's decision to pursue a career in acting. *Barabbas* is an interesting film in that it managed to capture Christ's crucifixion scene during a spectacular February 15 total eclipse of the sun.

Given the events that transpired in the life and death of Sharon Tate, there is unquestionably an enigma wrapped in a paradox when considering that her first movie role in *Barabbas* would be the decisive career-launching moment. For instance, there is something definitely mysterious about Sharon's life regarding the real-life murderer Barabbas. The real Barabbas in the gospels had his execution sentence commuted by Pilate.

Again, this is an example of another convergence of Sharon Tate with the mysterious workings of providence that could go unnoticed by aspiring writers. There are hints at angles of diegesis in building a spectacular Sharon Tate narratology. Almost every interpretation of Sharon Tate since her death is about the dark connections and these connections are convincingly written. Has anyone really put effort into tracing any of Sharon's bright connections? Sharon's story, even as it continues today, will experience an ending of some sort when everyone passes away who knew her personally or had anything to do with her life. At that point everyone will be left with only artifacts.

Writers and people who never knew Sharon should be able to continue working with the artifacts. There will remain

---

40 Columbia Pictures Corporation (1961). *Barabbas*. IMDb title tt0055774.

the millions of images, the many television appearances, biographical books, and movies. The movie *Barabbas* will always be the first cinematic artifact. In the *Barabbas* movie storyline, the fictionalized Barabbas continues his treasonous behavior upon release, eventually becoming a gladiator slave in the Roman coliseum. This is of course a what-if scenario applied to a biblical character. The now fictional Barabbas impresses Emperor Caesar enough by his arena fighting performances to receive what is an encore commutation to what Governor Pilate washed his hands of. This time, the commutation comes from none other than Nero himself.

There are arguably several additional similar parallels to Sharon's real story, which continue to affect our lives today. For instance, these corresponding events could make for a simply gripping Sharon Tate backdrop along the lines of Barabbas the murderer as it pertains to real life. Doing so undoes what journalism did by often placing blame on victims in the aftermath of Sharon's murder. Sharon's time on Earth makes for a screenplay literally bursting with life when seen from a Barabbas the murderer angle.

Likewise, there is plenty of action-packed Sharon Tate material for a writer to consider in romanticism, symbolism, imagery, themes, and settings. For instance, it is an oddity that in June of 1969 Judy Garland would die of a Seconal barbiturate overdose in London, England while Sharon was across town.[41] The 1967 *Valley of the Dolls* movie that Garland was fired from portrayed barbiturates throughout the script. One was make-believe and the other real life. A good writer could play upon this providential exchange in a docudrama format and come up with something unusually dramatic that maintains historical accuracy in the backdrop. Sharon just finished filming in Italy what would turn out to be her final movie *The Thirteen Chairs*

---

41 King, G. (2000). *Sharon Tate and the Manson Murders*. Barricade Books Inc. Fort Lee, New Jersey, United States. ISBN: 978-1569801574.

[42](titled *12+1* for its Italian release). Sharon was wrapping up shooting some of her parts for this film in London. As the film went into its post-production phase, Judy Garland died.

Sharon was now set to go home from London to Los Angeles in time for the baby's delivery. However, Sharon was so far along in her pregnancy that she was not able to take international flights and had to make the trip from Southampton, England to New York beginning July 11, 1969 onboard the brand new Queen Elizabeth 2 (QE2) ocean liner.[43] Unconfirmed witnesses to Sharon's voyage tried to narrow down that she bunked in One Deck, Cabin 1072 of the QE2, and then apparently flew from New York to Los Angeles. Travel time calculations put Sharon in Los Angeles on July 19 or 20, 1969. For instance, the launch of Apollo 11 occurred on the day of Sharon's arrival in New York City on July 16, 1969, yet Sharon was at her Los Angeles home in time to watch the Apollo 11 moon landing on July 21, 1969 with her family. Sharon and her unborn child were then murdered about three weeks later.[44]

Sharon was only 26 years old when she died. Given this set of facts, sequence of events, and strange happenings, we are now left with solving the puzzle of Sharon's paradox. The years and decades following Sharon's murder only embedded this paradox in the American psyche. To resolve an entrenched paradox such as this, we have to go back to the drawing board, identify where to apply research energies to fill in missing information to allow the development of hypotheses, and then test each of the propositions that the process evinces. The resulting output of this deliberative process has to be airtight if genuine paradigm shift is to have a chance to occur. It is fair

---

42   Compagnia Generale Finanziaria Cinematografica (1969). *The Thirteen Chairs*. IMDb title tt0065361.
43   King, G. (2000). *Sharon Tate and the Manson Murders*. Barricade Books Inc. Fort Lee, New Jersey, United States. ISBN: 978-1569801574.
44   Bugliosi, V. & Gentry, C. (1974), *Helter Skelter: The True Story of the Manson Murders*. W. W. Norton & Company, New York, New York, United States. ISBN: 978-0393322231.

to anticipate that restoring Sharon will at first be turbulent, somewhat like running the gauntlet.

The problem originates with the confounding variable identified earlier as the times in which Sharon Tate lived. As it is with the normal pattern of social development, Sharon's parents raised her in a certain way, and when she grew up she was on her own. As we will see, Sharon's contest with the trajectory of her life would cause her to draw upon her upbringing. The profession of acting for Sharon was in some ways an uncontrollable variable since she had to get her foot in the door somehow. At the same time, the moviemaking business was undergoing a disruptive ideological experiment during that time. The bigger picture is the moviemaking industry taken as a whole.

Although the passive MPAA system was better than nothing, it was considerably inferior to the active measures of the Hays Code. Graphic theatric depictions of the Manson murders would have been a direct violation of the Motion Picture Production Code and yet the MPAA would simply have given it a rating. The only connection between the two censorship endeavors was that both were aimed at managing the degree of explicitness allowable before a given production's release.

There were subsequent amendments to the Motion Picture Production Code through 1955, and the MPAA replaced it in 1968 as infractions became so numerous that they were unmanageable. Rather than increasing resources to combat the flurry of Motion Picture Production Code infractions, the cost was reduced by transferring enforcement to the MPAA rating system. The MPAA would then come under assault.

The presupposition that human beings are by nature inherently good in and of themselves seems to be the basis of the MPAA system that does not actively censor. The Motion Picture Production Code takes the position that active measures are necessary because the tendency of human nature is to gravitate away from inhibition toward irresponsibility. Some people refer to this as "progress." Contempt for morally lawful restraint is progress, but in the wrong direction. There is a gulf of difference between liberty and licentiousness.

Since the replacement of the Motion Picture Production Code with the MPAA, the ability of Hollywood to affect lives for the better has been brought into question if not to a state of disrepair. To demonstrate this, we can consider the example of two persons watching a movie where one of them feels uncomfortable in the presence of the other because of the explicitness of what is being shown. Many people can relate to this situation because they have experienced that uncomfortable feeling. If something is extremely intimate, and cinema thoroughly displays it, it is not very intimate anymore. There are better ways to convey intimacy occurring and therein lies the challenge to producers.

Apparently, the unrestrained or experimental view that prevailed throughout the culture of the 1960s was left to run its course in the years that followed. Today, most people consider that time period to be at best, passé. The impression we are left with is that we tried that approach to life and it simply does not work out so well all the time. Licentiousness defaces liberty.

There is overwhelming evidence that Sharon was maturing despite these times and that she appreciated what her normal upbringing gave her. Sharon wanted to honor her parents out of love for them. She was still exploring and learning what works and what does not work by trial and error from no detectable malicious disposition.

We cannot conclusively determine whether or not Sharon would have eventually rejected the futility of much of it because she died. However, we do know that having a child of your own typically changes your perception of the world in a profound way. That fact alone has not been captured well in cinematic portrayals and is relatively unexplored territory. We also detect relocation within Sharon's personality profile from her previous adventurous experience cataloging period to an intuitive judgment disposition period while maintaining introspection throughout the transition. A closer look at Sharon's life would find any of her imperfections manageable.

Confident in her appearance, insecurity still plagued Sharon in other ways throughout her acting career. Insecurity led Sharon to take risks in attempting to assuage those gnawing worries about accepting well-paid acting roles. Suddenly, Sharon's unborn child displaced all that uncertainty in her soul because her heart was filled with joy as a new family member was on the way. This development definitely brought Sharon profound happiness with life. She was aware of the people, things, and places around her to a degree. However, at some point all Sharon could really see or take interest in was her soon to be born child and this is how we can honor her and her murdered child best. This partially resolves Sharon's paradox.

In the aftermath of the notorious crimes committed, society was in the process of splintering or changing direction. Our justice system was beset with powerful ideologues that, among other things, found a way to thwart the enforcement of a trial jury's verdict. The death penalty imposed against Sharon Tate's murderers was one casualty among many from this ideological imposition. Surviving family members were reduced to the place of having to directly engage the authorities and the people responsible for Sharon's murder at one public hearing after another.

The fight for carrying out the orders of the jury in Sharon's case goes on to this day. It is corrosive to our system of law and Sharon's dignity to even entertain this situation for one moment more. In a criminal prosecution, a jury is the ultimate power in the universe. A judge can only append to the decision of a jury, and that, only in jurisdictions that specify that kind of power. The power of the judge finds constraint in that he cannot tamper, remove, or suspend any aspect of the jury's decision. The decision is final in the sense that the case does not require retrial, but any jury decision can always be appealed on a case by case basis. However, in the instance of first degree murder, the appeal has to beat the executioner. There was no case by case basis when the death penalty itself was struck down as being cruel and unusual. A culture of life will ensure the authorities are held accountable for carrying out the death penalty in a timely manner for premeditated murder convictions.

The aggravating factor involved here is that the appellate decision was also made retroactive. It was not a "from this point forward" type of decision. The retroactivity is what was unnecessary and it can and should be recapitulated so that the murder convicts return to death row as the jury ordered. It should not be forgotten that every case tried before 1972 in California that resulted in a death penalty conviction was struck down. This is essentially declaring in muted fashion that these cases were in effect mistrials, but only as to the penalty phase.

The only way that the system could strike down the death penalty would be to go back and reinterpret the Constitution in such a way so that it serves an ideological purpose that is in conflict with the Constitution. This ideological tampering with the Constitution's original meaning is abusive when adding to, or subtracting from. For instance, adding animal cruelty or political opposition as a death penalty offense is adding to the original meaning of the Constitution, and is just as evil as striking down the death penalty. Calling any of this "progress" is a slap in the face to justice. It is precisely because human life is priceless that the death penalty for first degree murder is the appropriate form of law.

As discussed in the Preamble, California's 1972 decision to strike down the death penalty is made possible in our system of law where there is a conviction phase and a separate penalty phase to a trial involving murder prosecutions. The penalty phase in these trials is only to address aggravating or mitigating factors involved in the degree of murder. It was still an outside imposition against the decision of the jury in Sharon's case as to the retroactive aspect, and this is where a legal challenge can begin so murder convicts face the executioner once again. The retroactive aspect to the 1972 decision is what is preventing closure. For this legal ordeal to go on as it has is indeed troublesome and seems to get in the way at times.

Yet the best course of action is to speak out and be aware of the ongoing uncertainty in our justice system or the legal status of Sharon's murderers in particular, and vote accordingly as a citizen. This completely resolves the paradox. We now have a statement of the purpose, a rationale, and outline of a full resolution to the Sharon Tate paradox without chasing rabbits down a trail. There is little doubt that a case such as Sharon Tate's helps to highlight where exactly the justice system needs to reconsider its options to remedy. The overall assessment is that this frustrated social and legal justice situation for Sharon is treatable but will be overcome by a greater outpouring of concern coming from Hollywood itself. That concern is better served by an emphasis on the life of Sharon, and not her murderers.

Getty Images / iStock.com / Huỳnh Thanh Thảo

"The Son is the radiance of God's glory and the exact representation of his being"

Hebrews 1:3

The Plan

Internal to Sharon Tate:

We can present a responsibly modest but action-packed depiction of Sharon Tate which is balanced and accurate that all walks of life in our society could appreciate. Sharon died at the age of 26. This works to our advantage for those instances where Sharon might have been immature, experimental, or just exploring the world during the course of her life as she grew and acted in various movie roles as part of her job.

    The plan is to portray Sharon in modes. In one mode she is toddler, youngster, and teenager. In another mode she is an innocent young woman exploring the world around her and in another mode, she has to take responsibility for making a living as an actress. Later, she takes a vow of marriage to a man, which is a joyful but responsible act of maturity, and this, too, introduces a new mode for Sharon. Her pregnancy becomes the most pronounced mode of any for Sharon and serves as the centerpiece for presenting a happy ending to her portrayal. She gives up her career to become a mother, for example. In all things, we can still face up to the fact that Sharon simply liked to have fun in all modes, albeit in different ways fitting to a particular mode. There is the natural Sharon, the fashion Sharon, and the professional Sharon to work with. These modes can all be based on factual information.

It is important to the plan to note that there is no indication that Sharon was given to excess and every indication she was remarkably disciplined in her childbearing responsibilities. Her experimenting and exploring should not be overdone as some would have it. By most accounts, Sharon Tate in real life is a lot like the girl next door. The plan here is to portray how Sharon learned from her exploration of the world as part of her gaining maturity.

The movies that Sharon starred in are to be referred to for what they are: Make-believe. To this day, this distinction about Sharon's make-believe acting work versus Sharon in real life remains confused in the greater American psyche. Several factors contribute to an aggravation of this state of public confusion surrounding Sharon. What should not be forgotten is that there is more to Sharon Tate as a person that's worthwhile lurking beneath the surface that the public is not very much aware of. There is also indisputable evidence that Sharon was a good person, friend, neighbor, spouse, and co-worker.

What the public knows about Sharon is almost entirely drawn from make-believe movies, which is really no basis from which to learn of her. What can be learned is that Sharon's real-life outlook on the world began to change significantly once she became pregnant. The plan is to show Sharon making movies as an actress, how she pops in and out of character behind the scenes on a movie set, and goes home from work at the end of the day. This scenario can be modified, but a real life recounting of Sharon as a person will help better delineate the real world from the make-believe in the public consciousness. Sharon in real life is nothing like the characters she played.

In the 1965 movie *Eye of the Devil*, Sharon was selected to play the part of a witch-like character in her first ever starring role; however, Sharon never practiced witchcraft in real life. She

THE PLAN | 115

had to follow the script given her as part of the employment contract secured by her agent. The *Eye of the Devil* movie was Sharon's first big break in the movie business and she fulfilled her commitment in playing the acting role given her.

To give you an idea of the significance of this development, before *Eye of the Devil*, Sharon had mostly television show characters to play and some very brief movie bit parts. The *Eye of the Devil* movie was later weaponized against Sharon after her murder, and it further traumatized the Tate family who knew her in real life. The journalistic reporting immediately after the murder wrongly accused Sharon of practicing witchcraft in real life. This compounded the already negative public perception problem by implying that somehow Sharon was a dabbler that contributed to her grisly death from poor judgment and bad company.

There were instances here and there of bad company, but nothing really out of the normal for a Hollywood actress. Sharon did not actively seek out creepy associations, but the actions of several individuals around her had some undesirable effects. Any accusations about the conduct of Sharon Tate's real life or unsubstantiated statements attributed to her are to be ignored as trite on the grounds that she is a murder victim and therefore comes under special social protection. The proposed plan is not an excuse-making formula nor is it a cookie-cutter approach that fits everyone to a tee, but is tailored for a person that had her life taken in such a way that it horrified hundreds of millions of Americans.

Depictions of dishonorable persons, unsavory associations, or graphic crime scene imagery concerning Sharon Tate will have to be censored for this kind of campaign plan to work. This will include removing Roman Polański until he makes restitution to the authorities for the crimes he committed in real life, or until he at least asks for forgiveness in public out of grief for what he has done. That kind of response from Polański has to proceed from a genuine sense of sorrow and that is what the law is intended to be good at eliciting. The cruelty inflicted on the victim's families by his flight from justice is extremely disturbing and our society should not be reconfigured according to Roman Polański's irresponsible view of the world. The desire for resolving this issue will have to come from Polański alone. It should be left to surviving family members to think about Sharon as an individual and stop there out of respect for victim's rights. As things stand, no plan with Roman Polański in it will survive first contact.

To include Roman Polański in an assembled image portfolio is an invitation for reproach and clearly an external force working against Sharon. This is not about being mean toward someone who was for a brief period a part of Sharon's fledgling family; rather this type of censorship is essential if any plan to focus on Sharon is to be successful. Sharon did her part and showed nothing but love toward Roman despite his behavior. One day, Sharon conceded "We have a good arrangement. Roman lies to me and I pretend to believe him."[45] Actor Laurence Harvey commented right after Sharon's murder saying, "Marriage vows mean nothing to him."[46] Discarding images of Sharon with Roman is without emotion and acts in our favor because Sharon is no longer married to Polański nor will she ever be in the future since no marriage is given in heaven.

Let us consider for a moment just how brief Roman Polański was part of Sharon's life. Sharon was married on January 20, 1968 and died the next year on August 9, 1969. That comes out to a little over eighteen months. Sharon lived about 319 months total, 18 months of which she was married to Roman Polański. That means that Roman Polański was a formal part of Sharon's life a mere 5 percent from the date of marriage to her death. If you want to count from the point that the two met it would be impractical to calculate, but if you included from the point she got engaged, it would make it about 7 percent. So, if we use a

---

45 Evans, Peter (July 24, 2005). *Sufferings of the Great Seducer*. The Sunday Times.
46 Ibid (2005). Actor Laurence Harvey as quoted by Peter Evans.

THE PLAN | 117

weighted averaging putting the figure at 6 percent to take all considerations into account, it seems a bit odd that after all this time, a campaign would risk everything by including any images of Sharon with Roman Polański at all. This is the 94 percent solution for portraying the life of Sharon Tate, while what has actually been done is stupefying: The event that took Sharon's life is about 99 percent of what the American public has been informed of about her life, even though it is less than .00000784% of her entire story.

Finally, as a rule of thumb, the few unnecessarily immodest images or media of Sharon are to also be discarded from Sharon's campaign portfolio. To summarize, all images of a crime scene, Manson or Manson Family murderers, Sharon with Roman Polański, or the handful of Sharon's portrayals which cross a clearly defined nudity boundary are to be censored out of consideration for the dignity of a murdered person.

Although at the individual level the boundary lines regarding what constitutes nudity differs, it is within broadcasting standards that about 99 percent of available Sharon Tate images will meet this particular portfolio selection criteria. Roughly 80 percent of Sharon imagery does not include Roman Polański. This makes the task of selecting acceptable Sharon Tate images for campaign portfolios easy to perform.

Part of this plan is to convince responsible individuals operating on the Internet to conduct open-source search queries for the millions of Sharon Tate images that are readily available. A dedicated individual can amass a great number of Sharon Tate images and apply these simple decision rules to determine which of them are to be included in the final set. There are further criteria set forth in the Annexes and Appendices to this plan.

One goal would be for individuals to build a highly respectable Sharon Tate image portfolio that prevents reproach and is easily shared on major Internet platforms. Naturally, the subject of Sharon Tate will elicit Manson Family-related reactions for many, because the public has been conditioned that way. However, individuals can become adept at side-stepping Manson or discussing Sharon's death and introduce much more wholesome information into circulation about Sharon's life in response.

External to Sharon Tate:

Our society began splintering but was not as socially and politically polarized in the 1960s as it is today. For those who have been around a while, there was a time not so long ago that we were not so much at each other's throats. Conservatives today who simply cannot stomach Sharon Tate for some of her liberal associations are rather quick to write her off wholesale.

Liberals who cannot stomach Sharon Tate because she failed to take up for liberal causes enough to their satisfaction will lack interest in her as a person that is to be held suspect as a closet conservative. The way it used to be, conservatives looked at liberal luminaries and agreed that they could not help but admire what they saw in specific liberals, and also understood that a conservative system would be unable to produce such outcomes. Conservatives were perplexed how liberalism as a system could yield such agreeably wonderful persons.

Likewise, liberals looked at conservative luminaries and agreed they could not help but admire what they saw in some conservatives and marveled at how conservatism as a system could produce such wonderful persons. In other words, we used to have a way to love one another without feeling violated in the process. In this way, liberals could remain liberals and conservatives could remain conservatives at the end of the day and yet respect one another's better halves.

This kind of friendly exchange between liberals and conservatives opened up lines of communication, fostering mutual admiration over time without giving up identity. At times, agreements were made to look past the major competing philosophical systems and join forces. Politically, the country managed to move forward in union with the best of both camps forging a single, shared direction that both socio-political outlooks produced. Something happened that caused both outlooks to lose stability.

An appeal for liberals and conservatives to put their differences aside for a moment and identify the qualities that they like in Sharon Tate can and should be formally conducted. It will become easier to see where the two camps diverge or intersect, and proposals to find agreement for joining forces on those points that intersect would become the main effort. The plan is to portray a balanced view of Sharon that preserves her dignity in a way that generates admiration from the general public. The basic idea here is to give no occasion to offending the sensibilities of either of the competing socio-political philosophies. Accomplishing resolution for forces external to Sharon Tate is difficult work.

It is interesting how a lot of celebrities who knew Sharon personally or had any connection to the places that she lived, worked, or was murdered seemed to almost run away in the aftermath of her murder. A lot probably went on behind the scenes. Some acquaintances have come forward since then from a latent sense of duty.

However, as the investigation and subsequent search for Sharon's murderers ensued, most of her celebrity acquaintances fell into one of two camps. The first camp wanted to make it known that they were at a party in Sharon's house, or were invited that evening but something came up. This camp had integrity issues. The other camp of celebrities was not stepping forward or speaking up because they did not want to be involved. Many associates of Sharon Tate are still alive today who have and could continue to work wonders behind the scenes in a new campaign effort would contribute in one way or another to reversing the current situation.

Given that so much time has passed and much of the threat removed, it is necessary that the plan considers forces external to Sharon such as debate-like discussion, images of crime scenes, results of criminal investigation work, lurid punditry, or anything about the perpetrators of this crime against Sharon. These counterproductive incidentals and images are to be ignored as unimportant and irrelevant. Time has worked to Sharon's favor regarding how we can go forward by presenting her life in a favorable light, and in a way not calculated to offend good people.

Sharon's former peers in the acting business can seek to find ways that redefine her in appropriately loving terms. This can occur from whatever angle they wish; not for the purpose of rewriting history but rather to bring her some form of overdue social justice. Whether or not the Internet plays a significant role in such a campaign, Hollywood as an institution can reassert its commitment to integrity by defending the dignity of Sharon Tate despite her long absence – a situation that cinema as a unique form of communication is well capable of doing.

There is an expectation that there will be unsung heroes in a campaign who would work hard to these ends. Unsung heroes instead find their treasure in heaven, and this is a sure reward for them when it is done for the purpose of giving glory to God alone. Current efforts would necessarily entail leveraging archived visual media in fresh or creative ways that avoids the temptation to exaggerate or mislead. Celebrities would likely bring the most clout via supporting narratives and calls for Sharon's ultimate vindication as one of their own.

Media is a powerful instrument in the hands of skilled professionals. Professional producers consist of the following four broad types: 1) level-headed, 2) completely indifferent, 3) recklessly provocative, 4) obstinate activist. All four types of professional producers are somewhat equally competent at their craft, competing against other professionals in the business. However, all four types can be made compliant using a different approach for handling each type. Control is maintained primarily through dollars and prestige. This plan takes the position that in the absence of the Motion Picture Production Code, the indifferent, reckless, and obstinate activist producers should be deprived of prestige. Media is to be a handmaiden to engendering good and not evil.

Visual forms of media can deliver the kind of raw power necessary to erase decades of intentional or unintentional wrongdoing in Sharon's portrayal. Several approaches to addressing the visual media problem in society are possible. A big-budget Hollywood production aimed at countering the negativism surrounding Sharon is the appropriate option. The flexibility within this option is somewhere between the individual Sharon Tate campaigner and the entertainment promotion levels. Individuals or small groups working on the cyber domain problem are able to penetrate society to its deepest levels, particularly when done on the one-to-one level. Production corporation promotionals working in concert with individuals tend to excite people working together on a campaign effort.

Shortly before her death, Sharon reflected upon her movie roles saying, "Sexiness is all in the eye of the beholder."[47] This was a summation of her catalog of experiences in life, yet today there is still a power of presence to Sharon Tate's visual media that serves as an external force for good, even though it exists in artifact. Disciplined beauty inspires exuberance or happiness in others and is for the greater good when done right. One way to look at the question is through a closer look into the metaphysics of beauty. There are many propositions for explaining what beauty is, but one of the more common understandings is the *objective* and *subjective* metaphysics of beauty.[48] For example, truth is objectively beautiful as a constant in a sea of change. Sharon is of a beautiful

---

47   King, G. (2000). *Sharon Tate and the Manson Murders*. Barricade Books Inc. Fort Lee, New Jersey, United States. ISBN: 978-1569801574.
48   McAllister, J. (1990). *Dirac and Aesthetical Evaluation of Theories*. Methodology and Science.

appearance in the eye of the beholder, which can vary. People can and do come around over time to how good of a person she was which is closer to the objective metaphysics of beauty continuum. To dwell on Sharon's physical appearance alone does not do full justice to the concept of beauty because she could have been a good looking, yet evil person. Sharon's full metaphysical identity is what the American psyche can objectively discover.

A good example of objective beauty would be Einstein's mathematical proof for the theory of relativity which takes hundreds of characters to communicate. When simplified to the $E=mc^2$ expression, there is something more to say about simplification than the laws that govern the ability of mathematical expressions to reduce.[49] Simplification of the complex has an objective beauty to it because simplicity tends to bring resolution such as Euler's Identity $e^{i\pi}+1=0$, enduringly considered to be the most elegant expression of objective beauty in human history.[50] What Euler's Identity expresses always existed in reality and Leonhard Euler only discovered the Identity. Likewise, Sharon's identity is discoverable.

No one is saying that displaying beauty in visual media is an easy task because it is an intricate process that makes metaphysical essences seem more concrete. The challenge for writers is to communicate Sharon's genuine objective beauty using the theatrical devices of plot, theme, suspense, intrigue, and comedy. The implied task is to carry the thought over to a study of Sharon Tate's disposition to do what is good, and emphasize those instances where her life intersects with the formal virtues. There is a way that Hollywood can unite for a moment to make something decisive about Sharon Tate with the intent to discover an optimum convergence of subjective and objective forms of beauty. The production would have to be something that is an honorable act of love and everyone knows

---

49   Lamouche, A. (1955). *Le Principe de Simplicité dans le Mathématiques et dans les Sciences Physiques*. Paris: Gauthier-Villars.
50   Euler, L. (1748). *Introductio in analysin infinitorum*. Lausanne, Switzerland.

it. Carefully presenting Sharon Tate can and should be possible in all forms of media as the vehicle. An analysis like this one is only a tiny beginning.

A great example of how to proceed was made by Gene Gutowski in the days following Sharon's murder. Gutowski had been following news accounts about Sharon practicing Satanism, witchcraft, illegal drugs, orgies, and other baseless speculation. Journalism's surveys of Sharon's acting roles grounded themselves solely upon the characters that Sharon played in movies to describe her as a person in real life. Somebody in a position to do something about it should have spoken up for Sharon at that point.

In order to communicate the vast difference between the make-believe nature of acting and real life, Gutowski as a film producer and close associate of Sharon Tate had to explain to investigative reporters at a news conference that he visited the scene of the crime and wanted to report that, "All I found there were sets of baby clothes. She was so happy, and ready to give birth to her baby."

"Beauty is in the mind of God, and the world is but a shadow of the divine image"

Saint Augustine

There is no Star for Sharon Tate on the Hollywood Walk of Fame

Getty Images / iStock.com / Meinzahn

Timing

There is a target of opportunity present for this campaign generated by the recent death of Charles Manson. Straight away, several Hollywood movie producers took it upon themselves to announce plans to make big-budget movies that would exploit the real-life horror of the Manson murders in ever more shocking detail. This approach caters to the barbaric instincts in all of us that civilized societies attempt to suppress by various means.

Such movies are nothing more than an appeal to negativism and it carries the wrong teaching effect along with it. The goal of timing in this plan is to alter the course of events in the arrow of time so that it halts or seizes initiative either in your favor or at least away from another. In the case of murder as entertainment, the goal of timing is to intervene against such movies prior to their release. The means of intervention are manifold but it has to be for the purposes of preventing a greater evil. Intervention against a moving wagon could be ramming, deflecting, blocking, or driving a stick through one of the wheel spokes.

The timing of these barbaric movies is transparent. In fact, an entire slate of Manson murder movies had release dates set for the same day that Sharon Tate lost her life, which also happens to be the 50th anniversary of this monstrous crime. This prevailing negative attitude should be condemned by free and responsible citizens everywhere and those productions responsibly torpedoed at first by entities that can impose lesser sanctions such as the Screen Actors Guild (SAG-AFTRA).[51] Persons of good report can also voice concern or objection to a greater degree when timing their responses for maximum effect.

Part of the contemporary problem is different than yesteryear. There is the new problem of people confusing make-believe movies with even less believable computer game plots. Recent crimes committed by youth seem to indicate that computer games influenced their confusing the make-believe with real life. It is not known if this is simple excuse-making and the question is under study by criminologists, but the computer game option for movie corporations would at least get the problem out of the moviemaking business.

What the more vulgar movie producers attempt to manufacture in cinema is probably better suited for cartoonish computer games, and any amendments to the Motion Picture Production Code in light of modern times would empower corporations to repurpose the more indignant movie proposals to that level. Why waste $100 million dollars on producing a movie that is only worthy of computer game status?

Computer game developers could have requirements to make their entertaining, but rather juvenile, games from the shooter's perspective, where countrified Sheriffs or trigger-happy National Guard troops lay siege to Manson's Death Valley Barker Ranch using helicopter gunships and tanks. Cartoon police armed with Manson warrants where the ink is not yet dry could be armed with large caliber pistols and pump-action shotguns to apprehend the bad guys. Digitally caricatured Highway Patrol police could have exotic ammunition selection options and even Rambo-style machine guns available for

---

51 Screen Actors Guild - American Federation of Television and Radio Artists (2018). 5757 Wilshire Boulevard, 7th Floor, Los Angeles, California, United States.

pursuing Manson Family getaway cars. High resolution graphics card SWAT teams could conduct massive raids and shoot-outs at Spahn Ranch as part of a domestic terrorist base camp sweep.

The almost demiurgic creators of computer game plots could go on and on with this line of thinking, ad infinitum. The idea is to eliminate Manson from movie productions by demoting him to the computer game world. Charles Bronson-type vigilantes could chase down Manson Family creeps showing up in respectable Hollywood neighborhoods with knives. Claymation action figures could hurl cartoonish spears through Manson Family groupies in the very act of an orgy. A bunch of ticked-off neighbors looking like an animated version of Grant Wood's masterpiece *American Gothic* painting could simply squeeze off night vision scope sniper rifle rounds from miles away into Manson Family zombies whacked-out on LSD around campfires. This sort of computer game gimmickry is mentioned here strictly as an example of how computer game developers could apply their skills in a way that it removes Manson from American life in the movies.

Some societies frown on the acting profession altogether as being an occupation that is on par with prostitution. The perception is unfair but good governance could identify areas of emphasis for improved perception. Actors have to make a living but the system should have more reasonable visual media content safeguards imposed on producers that helps protect serious actors and actresses working in their profession. Some movie producers, for less than honorable reasons, exploit actors and actresses who are seeking work. It is hard enough to pursue excellence in cinema without corrupt persons taking advantage of good natured people.

Moviemaking corporations could consider a repurposing approach to decision-making so that it helps prevent the possibility of professional actor embarrassment for their otherwise reluctant participation in a movie production that better belongs to a computer game format. Computer game designers would put the Manson Family where they belong: In a juvenile virtual reality world and it would practically all be done under the radar. For the betterment of lives, big-budget movie producers should all want in on a blockbuster movie about Sharon Tate's life instead. Generating demand would be an easy if not uplifting task for marketing departments, considering that there is an abundance of Sharon Tate images available to work with.

Nevertheless, it is reasonable to expect that actors will ignore any SAG-AFTRA censures against movies portraying Sharon's death because they can. However, having the public censure in place will formally convey an understanding that violation in this particular case will carry some form of negative consequence such as diminished levels of respect. Attaining actor union expressions of concern would be a middle-level goal. A campaign plan would greatly assist in synchronizing SAG-AFTRA's efforts with Hollywood movie corporations that are working in tandem toward the same objective.

On the brighter side of things, there is one movie titled *Tate* that seeks to focus on the life of Sharon Tate. The screenplay for the movie *Tate* has the approval and participation of the only remaining immediate Tate family member alive, Debra Tate. It is without a doubt that Debra, as a blood relative, was injured by the loss of her sister. Debra, as well as any good-natured person aware of the situation, would take offense at the continued exploitation of her sister's death at every turn.

The sole purpose of catering to depraved appetites is that the current state of affairs is allowing an avenue of monetary gain to materialize for the many sordid movie producers out there. As a glimmer of hope in the right direction, there is yet another endearing movie about Sharon Tate that is in the pre-production stages which might be able to go forward. This second movie that focuses on the life of Sharon Tate indicates that a campaign is already underway to portray her as a person worth knowing.

These developments are indications of combined momentum emerging in the area of professional cinematography.

The general idea at present is for future productions touching on the subject of Sharon Tate to have her somehow playing a living role despite her being unavailable to fill that role. Potential for achieving a greater good appears to exist in Sharon as a subject of consideration, given a logically linked campaign plan that plugs into that greater purpose. Sharon is therefore a candidate in need of a formalized campaign plan. At some point, arguably the present, a more detailed plan could be designed as the new and better course of action by competent persons to further celebrate the life and work of Sharon Tate.

Until a campaign swings into motion, Sharon will remain a mysterious figure who we never really got to know as a real person. There is enough information about Sharon's life for professional writers to examine as fertile ground for storyline conceptualization. Instead of writers and producers shunning the idea of Sharon being a subject worthy of consideration, they could have her appear out of nowhere in a new light, and in the process participate in a new dawn for Hollywood to the betterment of our lives.

This particular sketching of a Sharon Tate campaign plan addresses some aspects of risk mitigation for book or movie producers. It is understood that producers juggle limited resources as it is, so the reason for addressing the subject at all is to give producers a more common target to work toward. Each production will have its own level of contribution toward that common target. A more knowledgeable movie producer would be able to specify exactly what the flexible options are in a given production and more easily consider where to accept risk.

The way that this campaign plan lays out producer options is with the long-term in mind as a way of addressing the sustainability question. Treating the subject of sustainability will also facilitate the formulation of producer intent statements and how intent would feed into that sustainability. In the past, productions integrated sustainability into audio-visual presentations through the introduction of plot devices that leave the audience hanging in anticipation of plot resolution using partitioning, phasing, or installments. It is conceivable that Sharon Tate as a person is not only presentable to cinematic productions, but is also a billion dollar enterprise waiting to happen.

The real work is yet to be done and moviemakers would profit from concentrated efforts in the revised direction. The most kind-hearted of women have consistently been wonderful defenders of the dignity of good men in times of trial. However, men are relatively unskilled by comparison at defending the dignity of good women facing unexpected ordeals. The case of Sharon Tate would take skilled men and women working together to restore her to a proper and better place in the American psyche. The good news is that noble persons will have achieved a form of justice in her case and would not have to give up their integrity in the process.

This campaign plan is not intended for the half-hearted. As it stands, Manson murder advocates openly perpetuate downplaying or maligning Sharon Tate in particular because she is their soft underbelly and they know it. The explicit dramatization or even glamorization of these monstrous crimes against our fellow citizens by moviemakers is reprehensible. The only way to impart consequences to them in this situation is to ignore Manson or his murder advocates, and promote the life of Sharon Tate with supporting assistance from Hollywood's elites.

It is important to recognize that the availability of good people who can get things done is a relatively dwindling resource in our society. Top producers command top dollar and are absolutely expert in every aspect of their profession. It is expected that the men and women who share a desire to portray Sharon's sunny side would be on their best behavior and act as mature as they are motivated. Younger persons could look to Sharon Tate's campaign as a way for them to practice becoming more mature adults and it would also teach them how to handle difficult but solvable cases in the future.

The youth should have good examples to emulate. If you lose composure or convey a reckless portrayal of Sharon, it will reflect on you and negatively affect others working on the same thing. Thoughtful, imaginative conservatives and liberals are both capable of inspiring one another to preserve or advance Sharon's dignity in an uplifting manner. Sharon loved her parents and the people who contributed positively to her life.

Someone might find inspiration to write a more refined campaign for Sharon Tate after reading this and follow along with its inoffensive rationale, assessment, and plan regarding how best to go forward. Specific Sharon Tate issues can be addressed truthfully, straightforwardly, and gracefully. Again, timing is an important consideration in any effort to maximize effectiveness. There is about one year from the time of this writing to bring forces to bear on the problem.

There are several Annexes to this plan that address some of the technicalities deemed common to the present situation. Keep in mind it is easy to be negative, but difficult to remain buoyant over time in our world. Learning about Sharon Tate's life is a happy thing to know of, but learning about yourself and how you comport Sharon to others – should you so desire – is just as important. There will be temptations and disappointments with the world and it is understandable to disdain wrongdoing. Only a culture of life can restore Sharon and there is simply no way to do things right for her unless wisdom prevails. As for Sharon Tate, may the Lord bless her and keep her.

"Do not go gentle into that good night;
Rage, rage against the dying of the light"

Dylan Thomas

Getty Images / iStock.com / kdshutterman

Conclusion

This campaign plan serves many different practical functions. On the one hand, it is an attempt to make a one-stop shop reference manual when it comes to special social protection for Sharon Tate. There are two main efforts in view that occur simultaneously, yet their effects realized in sequence. The first effort is to achieve a steady state, defined by merely introducing something positive about Sharon's life into all forms of communication about her. The second main effort is to achieve a full displacement, defined as severance of the linkage between Manson and Sharon Tate in the American psyche. This plan serves as a media toolbox for the achievement of these objectives which serves the public interest for the betterment of the common good.

    Each individual that hears Sharon Tate's name will likely have a different set of predisposed thoughts about her that go into making the overall American psyche what it is, but this plan is written in a way that it is everything except another opinion. At the same time there is enormous value in the thoughtful opinions of others that would further the book's intent, or inspire writers in a similar fashion. There is a purpose statement, a rationale, a qualitative and quantitative assessment, working assumptions, and a plan designed from those considerations. The following is an executive summary of the result of this plan's deliberative process.

The plan identified three working assumptions that allowed the planning process to go forward: 1) Sharon Tate and the state of the American psyche are, and will continue to be in the public's interest for the foreseeable future, 2) long since entrenched disarray disrupting public policy will continue to frustrate the order of the jury to put Sharon's murderers in front of the executioner, 3) the culture of death that causes disarray will not give up power without a fight. The question becomes what can be done about the situation, and the first thing is to develop a plan that all stakeholders – media and citizen alike – can use.

The planning process was also able to yield three flexible options in light of these assumptions: 1) expose the motives, means, and methods used to exploit Sharon Tate in all forms of media which attempts to condition society to tolerate her degradation in public places, 2) explore Sharon's real-life trajectory when she died so as to form a reasonable future conjecture, 3) develop and propose targets for book writers and movie producers who promote the common good with Sharon Tate as the primary or significant subject of interest in a given production. Flexible options #1 and #2 are actions that anyone can undertake. Flexible option #3 is an action that anyone could undertake but it would require some degree of book writing or moviemaking competencies in order to provide the most helpful of contributions.

The planning process developed three actual metrics that provide concrete value to all stakeholders. Metrics initially focused on the ability to discover proportionality when considering the entire set of books and movies involving Sharon Tate. The first metric does not yield a quantitative value but it does allow a qualitative breakdown of the entire set of books and movies into the life, death, or steady state categories. The reason that this metric is qualitative is because a book or movie about Sharon would be either about only her life, or only about her death. However, a given production that mixes the two would fall into the steady-state category in almost every instance, which requires a more qualitative assessment. When comparing the books or movies about Sharon Tate that are purely about her life versus those that are only about her death, a quantitative metric can quickly portray the exact proportion that the public faces at any given point in time. The good that this metric offers is that we can track movement over time. We can also track volatility occurring within the steady state category.

Finally, the plan envisions an end state where there is severance of the linkage between Manson and Sharon Tate in the American psyche. At a minimum, the American public should know Sharon Tate more for whom she is and not what was done to her, and that is where promotion of the common good comes into play. The plan assesses that the resources to accomplish the betterment of the common good with Sharon Tate exist, but are in an embryonic state. To repair Sharon Tate's dignity is to increase public trust, and engenders the public entrusting institutional leadership with the power to achieve the aim of increasing public trust.

This girl, Sharon Tate, was born one day; she grew up and lived for a while. She loved boys, got married and then was expecting, but one day her life was taken by someone. Stunned by the savagery involved in this crime against her and her unborn child, people forgot about Sharon's life and the joy that she brought to others. This also happens to other people in the world but not nearly in the same manner. In Sharon's case there are a lot of presentable pictures, many of which she probably would not mind people seeing. Can you help? That is all I want to say.

Annex A

Methodology for Constructing a Deliberate Sharon Tate Image Portfolio

In the contemporary Internet practice, most people see an image and hit a share button. For Sharon Tate's campaign plan, this kind of approach only requires one to self-prompt for images of Sharon Tate on an open query. The drawbacks to this technique are that the campaigner is easily distracted by the repeated queries and there is little method to the madness.

As a result of the share button technique, commitment usually fades over time. Any individual attempting to monetize a collection of Sharon's images should be detected and exposed. All it takes is one impure motive or rotten apple to spoil campaign efforts. In summary, look for efficiencies in organizing open source Public Domain or Fair Use images of Sharon, do not attempt to monetize or commercialize without attaining prior authorization, act selflessly, keep others in mind, and have fun.

The simple share technique which most people use is better than nothing, but in order to sustain an effort, it is reasonable to assume that the committed campaigner would be vastly more organized and deliberate than this. The following is a proposed methodology for constructing a deliberate Sharon Tate image portfolio:

1. Not everything online is Public Domain. Always verify that Sharon Tate images in a portfolio are Public Domain or under Fair Use law. This is easier than it seems when there is zero commercial involvement, but the following Fair Use information is good to know: The image has to be for educational, scholarly, non-profit, non-biased, or research purposes and has to benefit the public as a whole. If in doubt regarding Fair Use as it pertains to a particular image because of where it was found, exercise prudence by conducting research until the answer is verified. Here is an example: When you visit Sharon Tate's *Wikipedia* page, only one image is *Creative Commons*, one other image is Fair Use, and all the rest are Public Domain. That means that most of Sharon's images on her *Wikipedia* page are portfolio assets because they are Public Domain. There are some citation requirements for most *Creative Commons* images usage. The *Wikipedia* images that have a requirement to cite have the exact citation handily included and you could make the citation part of the image filename. There are some other details that are worth knowing and some handy flowcharts available to assist people in being certain if a question were to arise. Public Domain type Sharon Tate images are what is what one typically encounters. On the other hand, a licensed image is a copyrighted image, and is unusable.

2. Dedicated Storage Medium. The bigger the better. An open source query for Sharon Tate images can turn up millions of images that are downloaded in bulk to a dedicated local space.

ANNEX A | 143

3. Scan for Metadata. A good portion of Sharon Tate images are blemished by watermarks and other undesirable artifacts. Images with metadata should be identified from a bulk download and set aside in a separate space. Any licensed images showing up in the image or its file properties should never be retained.

4. Group for Color. About half of the images of Sharon Tate are black and white, and the other half are color.

5. File Naming Convention. Naming files is arduous and the most time consuming, but a fast solution is to have a convention of some type that allows for query in the dedicated storage medium. As mentioned earlier, any citation requirement can be appended to a filename. The general idea is to be able to zero-in on an image that comes to mind as quickly as possible, so naming the image takes some forethought. The less identifiable the filename given the image, the more the need to rely on large thumbnail views in order to locate it in the portfolio. One helpful file naming convention is to suffix some of the images with "high resolution" and "sharp focus" or "soft focus" for those images that noticeably stand out as to quality. Another helpful quick organizing method is to suffix filenames with "Infant Sharon" "Younger Sharon" or "RARE", once you become familiar with how rare of a find it is.

6. Apply Decision Criteria. You can keep images in their various groupings, but images of crime scenes, excessive levels of nudity, and images with Roman Polański appearing in them should not be part of the effort and should be placed in an "unusable" folder space.

What is left is a working, dedicated campaign image portfolio. This will grow over time as the technique is repeated. The Sharon Tate image portfolio builder will notice an endless amount of new images available from these open source image queries. This is a sure sign that you are working with the ideal subject for a campaign and that this technique has the happy sensation of discovery associated with it. Introducing a Sharon Tate image on an Internet platform is usually enough to initiate a response and the campaigner can then go to work as a diplomat if necessary.

Experience has shown that the repetition of this technique can lead to the need for down time. Skipping the aforementioned minimum essential steps will work against you in the long term. Sometimes, the image discoveries are so interesting that you wind up realizing you wanted to take a break a long time ago but ever new images are what kept you going beyond expectation.

Studies consistently show that the average continuous human adult attention span is about fifteen minutes. As an average, this figure accounts for variance. However, the same test group population has about a *fifteen second* attention span when on the Internet. A dedicated image portfolio of Sharon Tate is going to be the most powerful instrument at your disposal given this reality.

Images have a residual effect about them that can make Sharon almost come to life in the viewer's mind. This should inform the image portfolio builder to take note of the power of media in general. Media is virtually indelible and it is a bit true that a picture speaks a thousand words. An accompanying narrative with the image can be helpful only some of the time, such as name, location, or interesting details.

Further image portfolio work would include organizing images according to significant events or places in Sharon Tate's life. This would take some familiarity over time to get it right. If there is any doubt as to the location or age of Sharon in a given image, then it is better to not take a guess and these can be left in a general folder. Integrity in building out Sharon Tate image portfolios generates respectability and operational reliability.

For those images that are verified as to their location, instances where other persons appear in the images, or the age of Sharon, take note of that substantiating information and consider if it would be helpful to add that information along with the image. Annotations to Sharon's images seem to work better if done infrequently and with an eye to brevity, so as not to distract.

As for dialog, it is not absolutely necessary to engage people in public, but if responding to written prompts, never give up your integrity for any reason to achieve goals. At the same time, temper what is said out in the public domain. None of this is to be construed as legal advice, but these factors are a consideration of the planning process. In order to maintain an appropriate level of security, it is important to be on the lookout for invasive or inappropriate questions as well as information-gathering efforts from unknown entities that should not be permitted to gain an upper hand.

Annex B

Techniques for Selecting Sharon Tate Images to Share

Discussion of various types on social media platforms can serve as inspiration for what images of Sharon Tate would be the most fitting to a given discussion in ways that would not cause a thread to go off topic. The Sharon Tate campaigner should attempt to sense the right moment to introduce an image of Sharon or begin a separate discussion thread. A given image of Sharon should fit the narrative in a thoughtful manner, so efforts in this area require a type of synchronization of the images to narratives.

Even though Sharon died a long time ago, an image of her takes away all of that distance in the viewer's mind. To really bring Sharon Tate to life in others is to captivate their imagination or view her in a new light. Campaigners can help guide others to that desirable outcome.

It should not be forgotten that there has never been anyone who looks quite like Sharon Tate. There may indeed be someone who looks like the spitting image of Sharon but such a person has never been found after dedicated searches. Even then, such a lookalike would probably not approach Sharon's personality, but that is where Hollywood could take over. Acting allows a look-alike to be more believable in the audience's mind via a script. However, this would require the unlikely instance of a Sharon Tate lookalike that is also capable of professional acting.

Internet platforms vary in their degree of media-rich centric accommodations. This narrows down somewhat which platforms would be the most ideal for the more ambitious Sharon Tate image portfolio campaigners. Negativism, as it is encountered, should simply be ignored. This is made easier with clearly defined goals and objectives. Happy or thoughtful commentary on Sharon Tate's images should be rewarded with an appropriate response.

Annex C

Use of Animation

One of the things that a Sharon Tate campaign would want to accomplish is to raise awareness in a new way. Given the reality of Sharon's death, we can somewhat overcome that problem in the here and now through the use of animation. Animation would bring Sharon to life more than still images would.

The only reason the campaign presented in this book focuses on Sharon Tate images is that if it were to focus on building an animation portfolio, it would necessarily constrain the subject matter to the movies that Sharon appeared in where the illusion of motion exists. Building a Sharon Tate animation portfolio as an accompaniment is a smart idea if the worker senses that viewers of Sharon's images still feel distant from her for some reason.

There are primarily two means of animating Sharon's visual information. The first is animation generators, but the drawback to this means of animation is that the builder first has to have motion picture material to work with. The advantage of animation generators is that the output is relatively lightweight in file size and will automatically play when encountered online.

The other means of animating Sharon is online shared videos. The drawback is that videos will not auto-play on open source platforms due to the security threat that videos pose. Most online platforms will quarantine videos set to auto-play due to security protocols. The viewer would have to manually tell the video player to start. Taking into consideration the fact that the average adult human attention span is fifteen minutes but the same group of people has a fifteen-second attention span when online, it is recommended videos be limited to a one-minute duration maximum. The ideal video duration is fifteen seconds, which severely curtails available video search results. Thirty-second duration videos are a good middle point.

Annex D

Opponents

Going into campaign mode will sometimes draw out opponents, but none seem worthy of your time. Many different people who knew Sharon described her as a vulnerable person, and visual Sharon Tate media is no exception. There will be image alterations encountered from time to time. To begin to address the issue of vulnerability, there are two initial determinations that can be made: 1) the alteration is a positive enhancement to an existing image, or 2) it is an attempt to malign. Malicious image alteration is usually easy to spot by people and dismissed as such, which actually works in our favor. Given the many other possibilities such as instances of poor taste in otherwise innocent enhancement techniques is going to be a subjective call.

In order to avoid misunderstandings, it is best to take the position that using colorization of original black and white images of Sharon is the only portfolio enhancement option available. In addition to this recommendation, the colorization technology applied to black and white images of Sharon should be built around industry standard Artificial Intelligence (AI) colorization. This standard works well in this instance because it is based on a uniform, objective means. Industry standard AI completely removes the problem of subjectivity. Any other means of enhancement, however interesting or well done it may be to some people, should be deemed an art form intended for purposes outside the immediate scope of this campaign plan.

Appendix 1 to Annex D

Sharon Tate Contingency Plan Identification

A *campaign* plan is usually of limited duration and is the derivative of a *concept* plan, the difference being the campaign plan's defined end state. Sharon Tate is the concept and the *campaign plan* defines its end state as the final displacement of Manson in the American psyche. An easier way to say this is that if I were to identify an end state, I would also have to be able to map how I would get from here to there. If I get a flat tire on my car, I have several options, but my spare tire is the pre-identified *contingency* plan that still allows me to get from here to there. I execute this contingency plan when the situation calls for it.

Let us consider the situation where a malicious attack occurs on the dignity of Sharon Tate. The human response to such a development is typically going to be emotional or a disorienting sense of befuddlement. The contingency plan pre-identifies this threat and the response to it as to first bring the credibility of the claimant into question, and then to question the integrity of the claim in light of Sharon being a murder victim which is the weightier matter. This weighing of importance is at its heart a moral consideration that empowers Sharon's defense.

The question is whether or not a malicious claim or a variant of it also existed in the past, and if so to find inconsistency particularly when verification requires two or more witnesses to corroborate a challenge. Another question to consider is the motive of the accuser. Sharon is to come under special social protection in light of being a murder victim, which supersedes almost any other consideration that an individual tries to interject. That does not mean to deny reality, but to suppress an accusation in favor of her status as both a celebrity and murder victim. Sharon's dignity suffered most of all from her murder but also from inattention to her defense in the ensuing decades. The Sharon Tate concept plan is a snapshot of her entire life of which her final status as a murder victim takes precedence.

A campaign plan usually involves an associated timeline. Accordingly, the concept plan never dies but is also able to convey how a huge implied task in a campaign would break down into separately actionable pieces. Each constituent part will have clear linkages to the concept plan from which it derives but there may or may not be strong linkages between each constituent piece.

An example of how a campaign plan is highly beneficial could be in its resemblance to the theory of the business firm. If I look at the firm from a functions angle, I notice there are typically a production function, a marketing function, and a financial function at a minimum. All three functions work together and are necessary to the firm's operation in this example, but now I can exhaustively look at each these functions to the exclusion of all else. If I isolate the financial function of the firm then my perspective is now everything financially related to the operation of that firm. I can look at the constituent pieces of a campaign plan in the same manner.

Task complexity tends to increase as each constituent piece of a campaign plan initially undergoes an isolated examination. For instance, in the preceding example, the production function of a firm involves many separate tasks. A threat to accomplishing production could be a breakdown in the machinery essential to production continuation. Likewise, writing a screenplay for portraying Sharon Tate's life consists of many different supporting tasks. The campaign plan will not generally specify the minutia of individual tasks.

There are an infinite number of variables one could consider when identifying and examining threats requiring a contingency plan that ensures campaign plan accomplishment. It would be nice if we could take every single threat to the campaign and make one giant contingency plan out of them, but this is utterly impractical. If I get a flat tire, my contingency plan gets pulled off the shelf and it tells me not to call the tow truck but to swap the spare tire for the flat tire, which then allows me to get to where I am heading. The key point to the contingency plan is that it already considered all of the options at length beforehand, and decided upon what option to exercise. In summary, we have a *concept plan* (undefined end state and timeless), a *contingency plan* or set of contingency plans (addresses only the significant anticipated threats), and a *campaign plan* (a defined end state). The contingency plans stand-by for use as the campaign plan swings into motion.

In a perfect world, every real or possible obstacle to task accomplishment would have a separate contingency plan designed to effectively address each and every anticipated threat. The decision-maker would then draw upon the appropriate contingency plan at a point in time to know exactly where and how much energy to apply in mitigating or defeating a given threat, should it emerge. However, the constraint on contingency plans is that they should only address how the campaign plan would continue in light of the emergence of a pre-identified threat.

Contingency plans can go so far as to address specific nuisances, but this is not a substantive problem: Limited resources prevent the development of unlimited contingency plans. However, identifying the greatest or most significant threats to a campaign is indeed possible as to expectation of occurrence. These considerations guide the decision to develop the individual contingency plans. Contingency plans are beneficial because they pre-identify responses to the most serious and expected challenges. The contingency would ideally commit resources in such a way so that minimum effort would be necessary to remove the obstacle causing task impedance.

An example of this would be an anticipated challenge such as the spreading of disinformation by an opponent. This campaign plan takes the position of non-confrontation unless absolutely necessary. If done right, the contingency plan rightly anticipated the potential emergence of interference and the contingency already identified the appropriate alternatives available for the appropriate response. For example, the contingency plan presents a proven method of bypass or in the case of unavoidable confrontation, identification of the party responsible for the interference occurs.

Another example would be a no-win situation such as an Internet platform that no longer supports posting images. In this example, the contingency plan already identified at what point to enter into diplomatic negotiation so that negotiation becomes the contingency. Should insurmountable obstacles appear, opponents become intractable or fail to enter negotiation in the no-win situation as their tactic, the contingency plan outlines the path of least resistance in going forward. The contingency could outline a break out of some kind that allows for goals and objective accomplishment by other means.

Since we just witnessed fifty years' worth of unintentional suppression of the truth about Sharon Tate's life, identifying the methods employed by unhelpful portrayals as well as her outright enemies in the past can inform us of what to expect in the future. This campaign plan envisions a set of Sharon Tate contingency plans in the current operating environment. The number of contingency plans to develop depends on identifying a cutline in a listing of all identified threats. A contingency plan is written for each threat above where the cut line falls in the listing. Each contingency developed addresses each threat above the cutline in a way that it only supports achieving overall campaign accomplishment. In this way, when a significant threat does materialize, the ability to initiate a contingency plan exists. This campaign plan proposes brushing aside any lesser threats that do not actually interfere with campaign accomplishment.

A contingency plan could even go so far as building a flowchart that identifies the proper response for each and every effect that socially maligns Sharon Tate in some way. The contingency plan flowchart would then serve as a reliable quick reference where all the pre-thinking work occurred beforehand. Contingency plans above a cut-line of all possible threats would most likely place the impugning of Sharon's character above that cut-line and a detailed contingency plan written for that threat.

One of the first contingency plans under consideration should be notification of a new movie production that glorifies Manson or portrays without restraint the various murders committed by the Manson Family. The contingency plan can outline what steps to take that will lead to an effective intervention. As a plan, *"Sharon Tate Contingency 1"* should include what actions will lead to the development of a movie that will portray Sharon's life in a manner worthy of her. Thwarting a movie unfavorable to upholding Sharon Tate's dignity only allows the steady state. The production of a movie exclusively favorable to Sharon's dignity is the displacement. One alternative in a contingency plan would be to take a movie in production that is unfavorable to Sharon's dignity and cause it to become a movie favorable to her dignity.

Appendix 2 to Annex D

The following standalone electronic resources at the time of this publication meet the following minimum essential criteria of 1) adequate preservation of human dignity for a murder victim, 2) active online presence monitoring defined by at least monthly review and updating, 3) active purging of obscene, indecent, and profane content in accordance with the Federal Communications Commission's consumer guide definition, 4) cooperation with law enforcement when requested, 5) third party non-disclosure, 6) detection and noncooperation with interactive Manson murder advocates, and 7) effective participant risk mitigation controls such as adequate site security and deletion powers based on a system of diminishing goodwill. In addition to these considerations, this resource listing includes resources provided by reputable media outlets as well as the immediate living family members of Sharon Tate.

The Official Sharon Tate Fansite
http://www.sharontate.net/home.html

TMZ http://www.tmz.com/

CMG Worldwide
https://www.cmgworldwide.com/sharon-tate/

Wikipedia https://en.wikipedia.org/wiki/Sharon_Tate

Sharon Tate IMDb
https://www.imdb.com/name/nm0001790/

The Sensational Sharon Tate Blog
http://sensationalsharontate.blogspot.com/

Dave Draper
https://www.davedraper.com/dd/2017/05/07/memory-of-sharon-tate/

https://authormichaelawalker.blogspot.com/

https://www.facebook.com/tatebooks.georgesmith

https://georgevreelandhill2010.wordpress.com/2014/07/16/sharon-tate-recollection/

https://www.pinterest.com/georgevreelandh/sharon-tate/

https://www.flickr.com/photos/georgie56/16804278132/

"Two qualities are indispensable: first, an intellect that even in the darkest hour retains some glimmerings of the inner light which leads to truth; and second, the courage to follow this faint light wherever it may lead"

Carl von Clausewitz

Index

A

active control measures 58
agenda 17, 19, 20, 39, 93
allure 21, 30, 38, 64
American experience 30, 96
American Gothic 129
American psyche 14, 16, 30, 57, 63, 64, 78, 81, 103, 114, 122, 132, 137, 138, 139, 152
analysis 15, 40, 46, 47, 51, 82, 96, 123
animation 46, 148
Aquitaine 93, 98, 99
Archer, William 59
Artificial Intelligence 150
attention span 144, 149
authorities xii, 14, 24, 26, 27, 28, 29, 82, 83, 94, 96, 106, 107, 115

B

Barabbas 88, 101, 102
barbarian 21, 48
barbiturate 102
basis 37, 38, 40, 41, 42, 45, 83, 93, 94, 104, 106, 107, 114
beauty 1, 2, 50, 81, 121, 122
Borgnine, Ernest 101
brevity 15, 27, 145
broadcast standards 97, 99
Buckley, William F. Jr. 60
budget 27, 64, 78, 99, 100, 121, 127, 130
Bugliosi, Vincent 24, 35, 36, 39, 40,

C

Caesar 102
California 2, 23, 24, 25, 26, 27, 28, 52, 107
California Attorney General 26
California Attorney General's Office 26, 27
campaign plan 13, 17, 30, 48, 51, 57, 59, 62, 63, 73, 75, 79, 80, 84, 87, 92, 95, 115, 130, 131, 132, 137, 141, 151, 152, 153, 154, 155, 156
cataloguing of experiences 88, 89
cause 22, 30, 38, 57, 104, 146, 156
celebrity 6, 73, 77, 83, 84, 95, 119, 153
censorship 76, 77, 78, 104, 116
charity 16, 19

Château de Hautefort 60, 93, 94
checks and balances 80
closure 46, 108
colorization 150
communism 39
compelling interest 27, 100
complex problem 15, 58
concept xiii, 17, 36, 59, 74, 77, 80, 92, 122, 152, 153, 154
concept plan 152, 153, 154
conditioned to tolerate 79
conditioning 17, 79
confession 28
confounding variable 44, 96, 104
consciousness 26, 37, 114
conservatives 118, 119, 133
conspiracy 13, 24, 74
Constitution of the State of California 23
Constitution of the United States 23, 26
constraint 18, 106, 154
contingency plan 152, 154, 155, 156
continuities 87, 97
counterculture 2, 16, 18, 19, 36, 37, 38, 39, 40, 51
countermeasures 96
counterterrorism 26, 27
courtroom theatrics 48
Creative Commons 142
culmination 74
culture 2, 5, 18, 19, 79, 84, 105
culture of death 15, 16, 17, 19, 20, 21, 25, 26, 29, 30, 38, 49, 50, 58, 63, 64, 94, 95, 138
culture of life 17, 29, 83, 107, 133
Culver City, California 51
cyberspace 58

D

Dallas, Texas 1, 23
death penalty 23, 24, 25, 26, 27, 106, 107
Death Valley 128
decision authority 23, 62, 77
degradation 17, 19, 29, 51, 52, 64, 82, 138
deliberate 20, 62, 77, 141, 142
deliberative planning process 58, 138
Department of Homeland Security 83
devaluation of human life 39
Diderot, Dennis 59
dignity xi, xii, 14, 29, 31, 48, 61, 69, 73, 74, 81, 99, 100, 106, 117, 119, 120, 132, 133, 139, 152, 153, 156, 157
disarray 24, 26, 29, 63, 95, 138
discontinuities 87, 97
documentaries 75
domestic terrorism 83
drugs 2, 19, 20, 22, 36, 39, 44, 123
due process 26, 29
duration 16, 149, 152

E

effect xii, 6, 22, 23, 24, 63, 81, 82, 96, 107, 127, 128, 144, 156
end state 30, 65, 80, 82, 139, 152, 154
epicenter 3, 15
eroticism 60
Euler's Identity 122
event sequencing 43
evil xii, 15, 16, 17, 21, 40, 47, 58, 81, 94, 107, 121, 122, 127
evil twin 16, 17
executioner 63, 107, 138
explicitness 99, 101, 104, 105
exploitative 17, 59, 75, 79
Eye of the Devil 93, 98, 114, 115
eyewitnesses 41

F

factors 47, 65, 107, 114, 145
facts 18, 26, 29, 103
Fair Use 141, 142
families 6, 38, 39, 45, 47, 116
feasibility 43, 57, 62, 73
Filmways 88, 97, 98,
formalized 58, 63, 64, 97, 131
framework 38
functions 137, 153
funding authorities 27, 28

G

Garland, Judy 100, 102, 103
general public xiii, 14, 18, 36, 48, 59, 100, 119
generational divide 39, 95
Gilbert, Nora 77
goal 57, 63, 82, 95, 117, 127, 130
Golden Era of Hollywood 80, 95
Gutowski, Gene 123

H

Harvey, Laurence 116
Hays Code 76, 77, 78, 79, 80, 81, 96, 99, 100, 104
Hays, Will 76, 77, 78
Hefner, Hugh 60, 61
Helter Skelter 94
Highway Patrol 128
hippies 5, 18, 36, 37, 38, 39, 40
Hollywood xii, xiii, 1, 2, 3, 6, 8, 50, 51, 58, 62, 64, 69, 73, 75, 76, 77, 78, 79, 80, 81, 82, 83, 87, 88, 91, 92, 95, 96, 97, 98, 99, 100, 101, 105, 108, 115, 120, 121, 122, 127, 129, 130, 131, 132, 146
homicidal choice 20, 21, 95
homicide 25, 28, 29
human life amendment 26, 27

humanism 19, 20, 38, 60, 61
hypothesis 42

I

ill-defined problem 58, 59, 80
imagery 57, 93, 102, 115, 117
immodesty 83, 99
implied task 122, 153
indicators 62, 88, 91
information xii, 16, 40, 42, 43, 45, 46, 47, 49, 63, 78, 103, 114, 118, 131, 142, 145, 148
innocence 15, 16, 21, 30, 31, 50, 51, 79
institution 25, 40, 60, 69, 78, 80, 96, 120
intentional homicide 23, 24, 28
interim remedy 27
Internet 4, 49, 117, 120, 141, 144, 147, 155
introspective 50, 59, 87, 88, 89
Italy 2, 8, 88, 93, 101, 102

J

Jewel of the Périgord 94
Johnston, Eric 78
joint taskforce 26, 28
journalism 48, 93, 96, 102, 123
Julien's 59
jury 24, 27, 48, 63, 106, 107, 138

K

known 5, 24, 31, 42, 44, 46, 48, 50, 59, 62, 74, 79, 81, 84, 93, 95, 119, 128
known known 43, 44, 46, 58, 63
known unknowns 43, 58, 63

L

League for Decency 99
liberals 118, 119, 133
Liesl 98

London, England 90, 102, 103
Los Angeles xii, 3, 5, 23, 28, 59, 103
Los Angeles District Attorney's office 23, 28
Louis XIV 93
LSD 129

M

main effort 75, 81, 119, 137
major media 19, 51
make-believe 65, 96, 100, 114, 123, 128
Manson, Charles 3, 5, 13, 25, 127
Manson Family 5, 14, 28, 30, 42, 48, 81, 82, 83, 93, 94, 117, 129, 130, 156
media 5, 17, 19, 28, 48, 51, 57, 58, 64, 65, 83, 87, 93, 117, 120, 121, 122, 123, 129, 137, 138, 144, 146, 147, 150, 157
Mephistophelian 20
metaphysics of beauty 121, 122
metric 92, 138, 139
mismatches 40, 42, 43
Mister Ed 97
modesty 83, 99
Motion Picture Producers and Distributors of America 76
Motion Picture Production Code 76, 78, 101, 104, 105, 121, 128
moviemaking 82, 91, 96, 104, 128, 129, 138
MPPDA 76
murder 3, 6, 13, 16, 18, 21, 22, 24, 25, 26, 27, 28, 29, 40, 41, 46, 57, 64, 73, 74, 77, 82, 83, 87, 94, 96, 98, 102, 103, 106, 107, 115, 116, 119, 123, 127, 132, 152, 153, 157
murderers 14, 17, 18, 20, 22, 23, 25, 29, 39, 40, 41, 42, 43, 44, 45, 48, 49, 63, 81, 82, 106, 108, 117, 119, 138

N

Nero 102
new dawn 14, 31, 80, 95, 131
New York 4, 103
nudity 117, 143

O

objective 42, 51, 81, 94, 121, 122, 130, 151, 155
Old Hollywood 95
opponents 25, 150, 155
optics 81
outcome 20, 28, 77, 146
outlook 18, 21, 37, 39, 81, 83, 91, 114
output 43, 103, 148

P

paradox 59, 73, 101, 103, 106, 108
parole 23, 24, 63
perception 16, 39, 44, 45, 91, 93, 105, 115, 129
personality 40, 50, 59, 78, 87, 88, 89, 91, 105, 146
phasing 132
philosophy 19, 25, 29, 30, 36, 38, 39, 59, 60, 61
physical evidence 29, 41, 42, 45, 46
Pilate 101, 102
Playboy philosophy 60
Polański, Roman 2, 14, 93, 115, 116, 117, 143
political 26, 37, 38, 39, 76, 107, 119
portfolio 57, 89, 93, 116, 117, 141, 142, 143, 144, 147, 148, 150
preliminary considerations 57
preventative measures 18
prioritizing 46
processes 43, 64
public awareness xii, 21, 27, 92
Public Domain 141, 142, 145

public interest 27, 93, 137
public trust 78, 80, 139
purpose statement 57, 137

Q

QE2 103
qualitative 91, 137, 138, 139
quantification 44, 92
Quinn, Anthony 101

R

Ransohoff, Martin 88
rationale 73, 80, 81, 82, 84, 87, 108, 133, 137
ratios 30
referendum 24, 25
religious humanism 20
resources xii, 18, 57, 93, 97, 104, 131, 139, 154, 155, 157
retribution 14, 16, 29, 48
retroactive 24, 25, 27, 107, 108
risk mitigation 131, 157
risks 18, 99, 106
romanticism 41, 42, 102
Rumsfeld, Donald 58, 59

S

Sacramento, California 27
SAG-AFTRA 128, 130
sanctity of life 20
scope 46, 73, 129, 151
situation ethics 18
social protection 74, 77, 82, 115, 137, 153
socialists 37
solution xiii, 15, 23, 25, 27, 28, 29, 41, 52, 117, 143
Southampton, England 103
special inquiry 27
stability 88, 89, 119

state constitutional amendment 24
State of California 23, 24, 25, 26, 27
state's evidence 41
steady state 30, 59, 92, 137, 138, 139, 156
Stockholm syndrome 15
sustainability 131, 132
symptoms 19, 21

T

taskforce 26, 27, 28, 12
Tate family 2, 28, 115, 130
Tate, Debra xiii, 130
Tate, Doris xiv, 1, 6, 30, 62, 90
Tate, Sharon xi, xii, xiii, xiv, 1, 3, 4, 5, 6, 7, 8, 13, 15, 16, 17, 20, 21, 22, 23, 25, 27, 28, 29, 30, 31, 35, 40, 46, 47, 48, 49, 50, 51, 52, 57, 58, 59, 60, 61, 62, 63, 64, 65, 69, 73, 74, 75, 76, 77, 79, 80, 81, 82, 84, 87, 88, 89, 91, 92, 93, 94, 95, 97, 98, 100, 101, 102, 104, 106, 113, 114, 115, 117, 118, 119, 120, 121, 122, 123, 127, 130, 131, 132, 133, 137, 138, 139, 141, 142, 143, 144, 145, 146, 147, 148, 150, 152, 153, 154, 155, 156, 157,
television 1, 35, 40, 48, 57, 88, 97, 98, 102, 115
The Beverly Hillbillies 1, 97
Motion Picture Association of America 77, 78
The Sound of Music 98, 99
The Thirteen Chairs 90, 102
theft of innocence 16, 21, 50, 79
thesis 15
threat 20, 39, 45, 120, 149, 152, 153, 156
timeline 43, 45, 153
timing 127, 128, 133
transition 58, 87, 89, 91, 106

U

unknown 46, 59, 62, 76, 91, 145
unknown unknowns 43, 58, 63

V

Valley of the Dolls 1, 4, 6, 99, 100, 102
variance 44, 45, 144
videos 149
visual portfolio 57, 93
vulnerable 21, 22, 50, 61, 150

W

Walk of Fame 51
Washington, DC 26
Weather Underground 28
wicked problem 58
wisdom 30, 78, 133

Y

yippies 18

Z

zealous 37

www.ingramcontent.com/pod-product-compliance
Lightning Source LLC
Chambersburg PA
CBHW041503010526
44118CB00001B/2